SKULLS

&

TRIPPIN' SNEAKS

COLORING BOOK

2 BOOK BUNDLE

SKULLS
Coloring Book

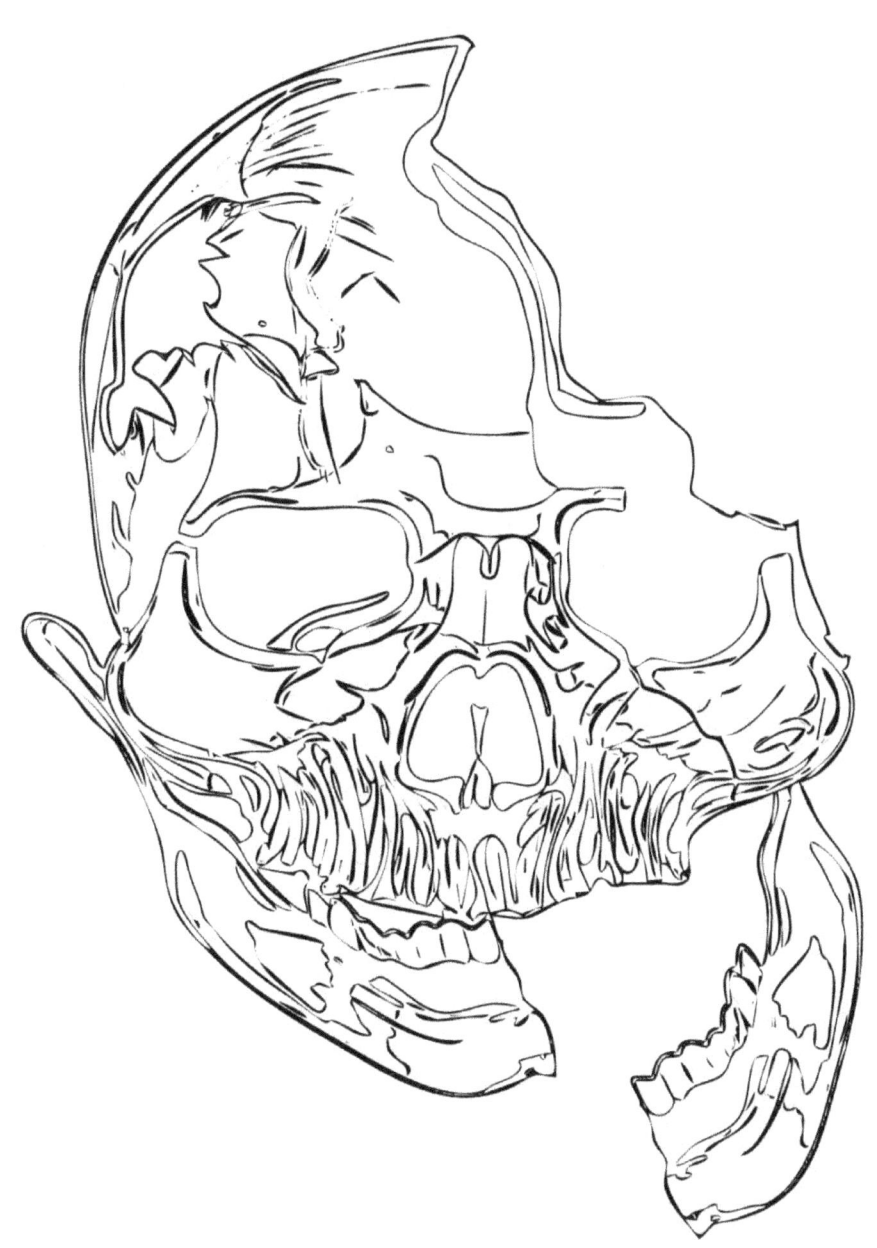

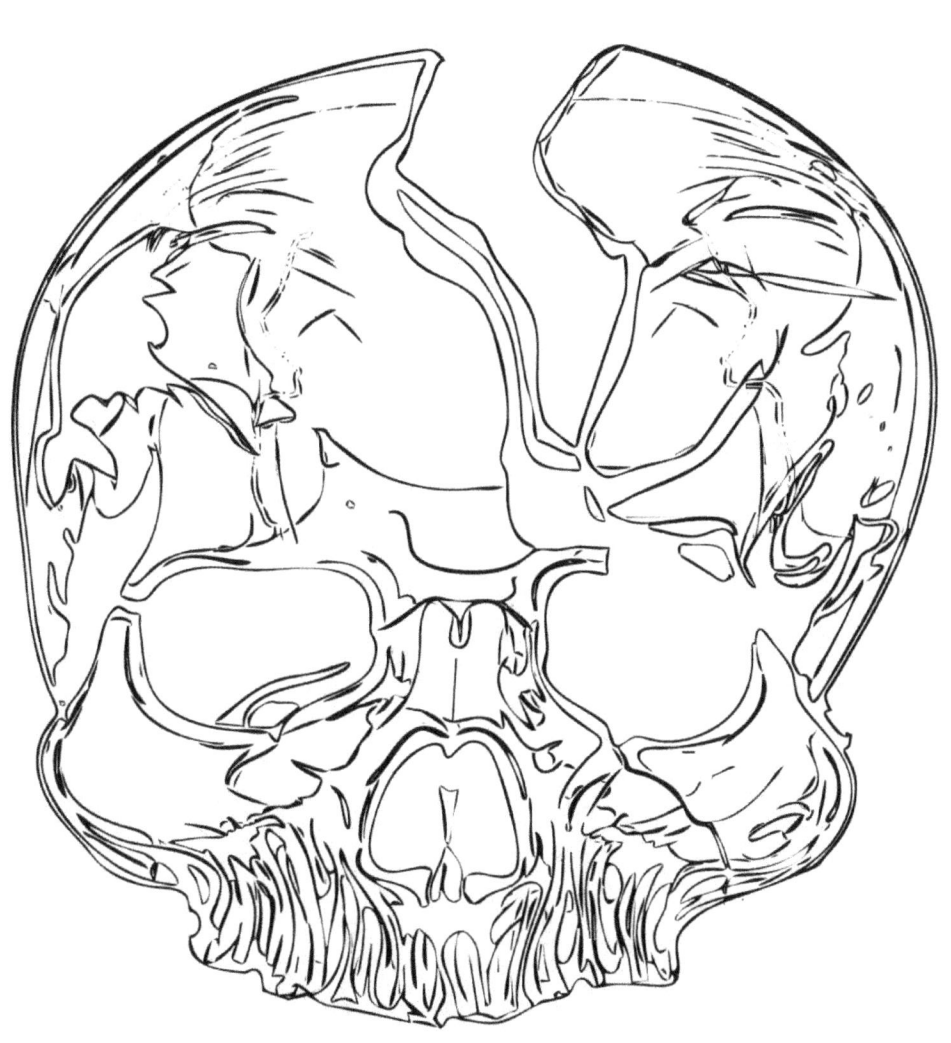

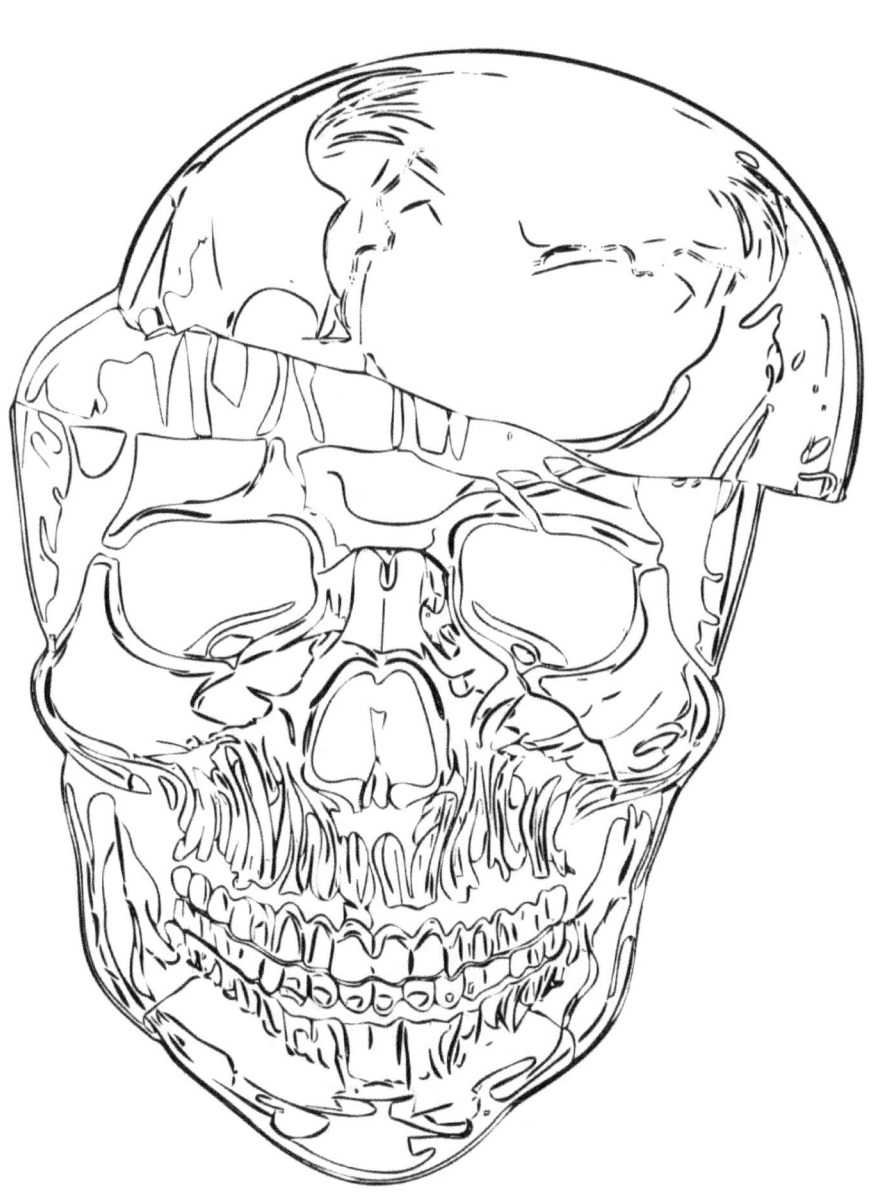

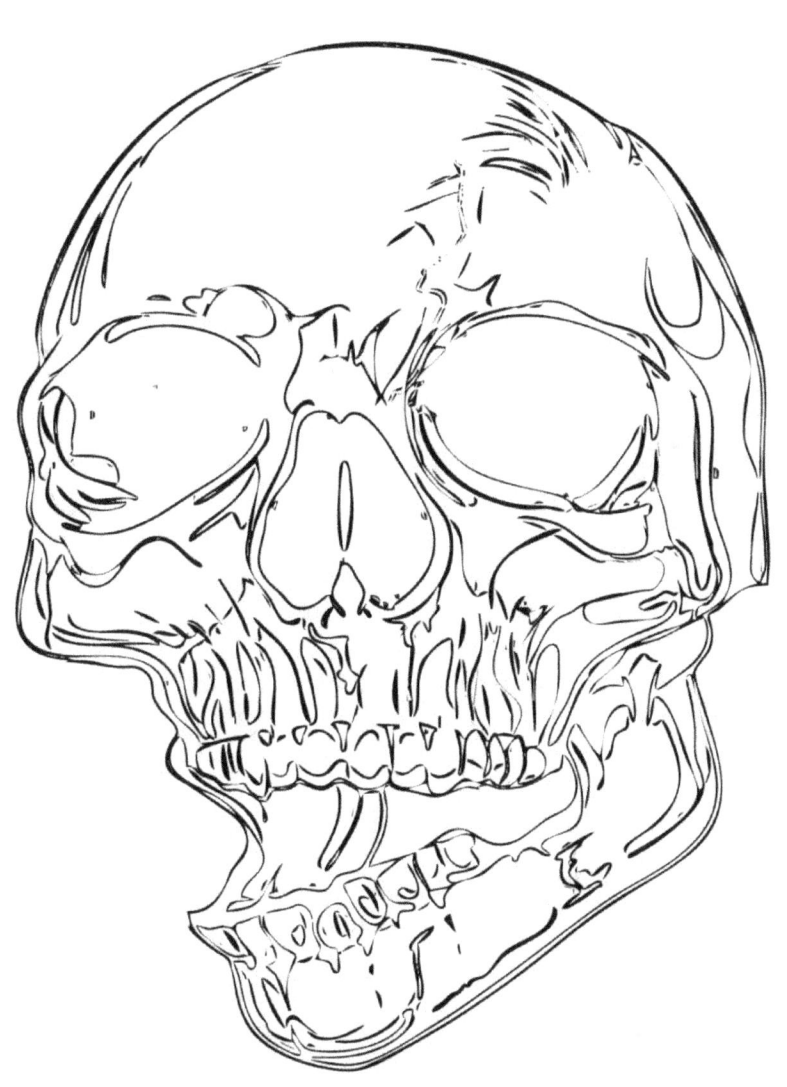

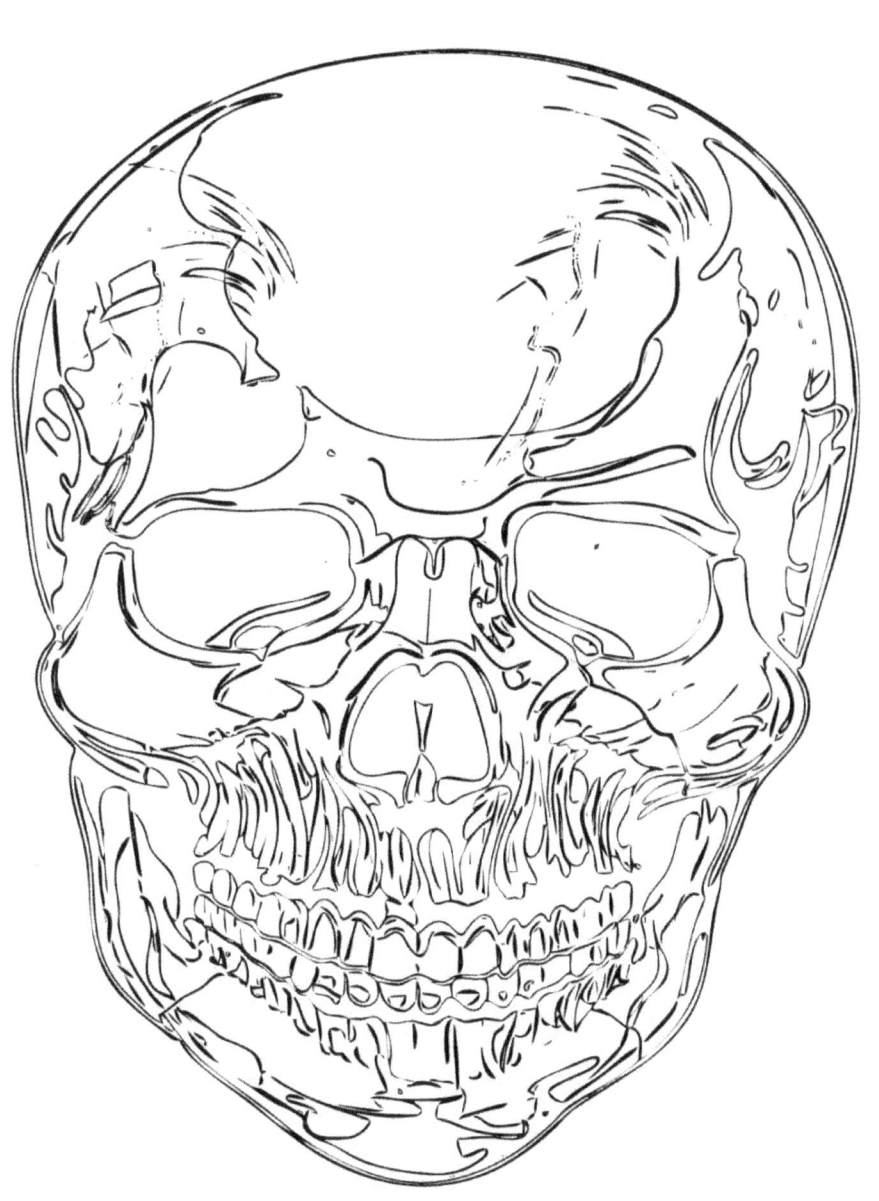

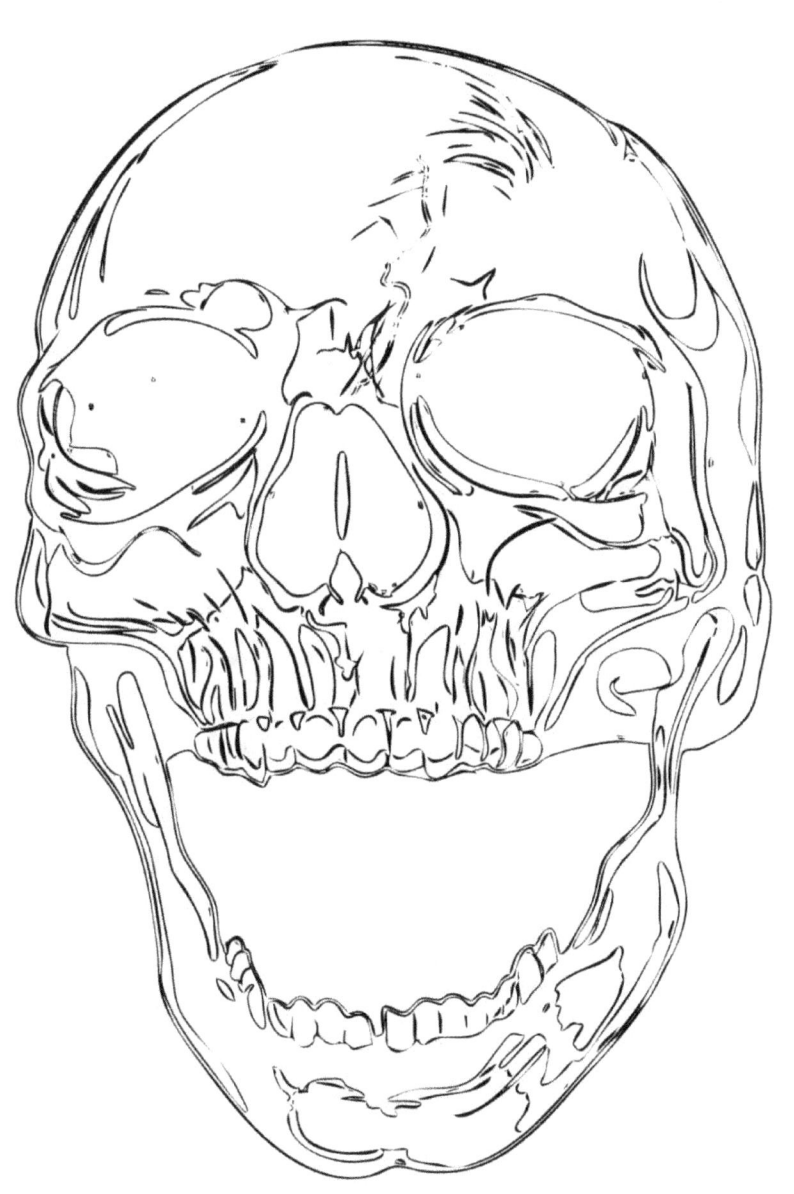

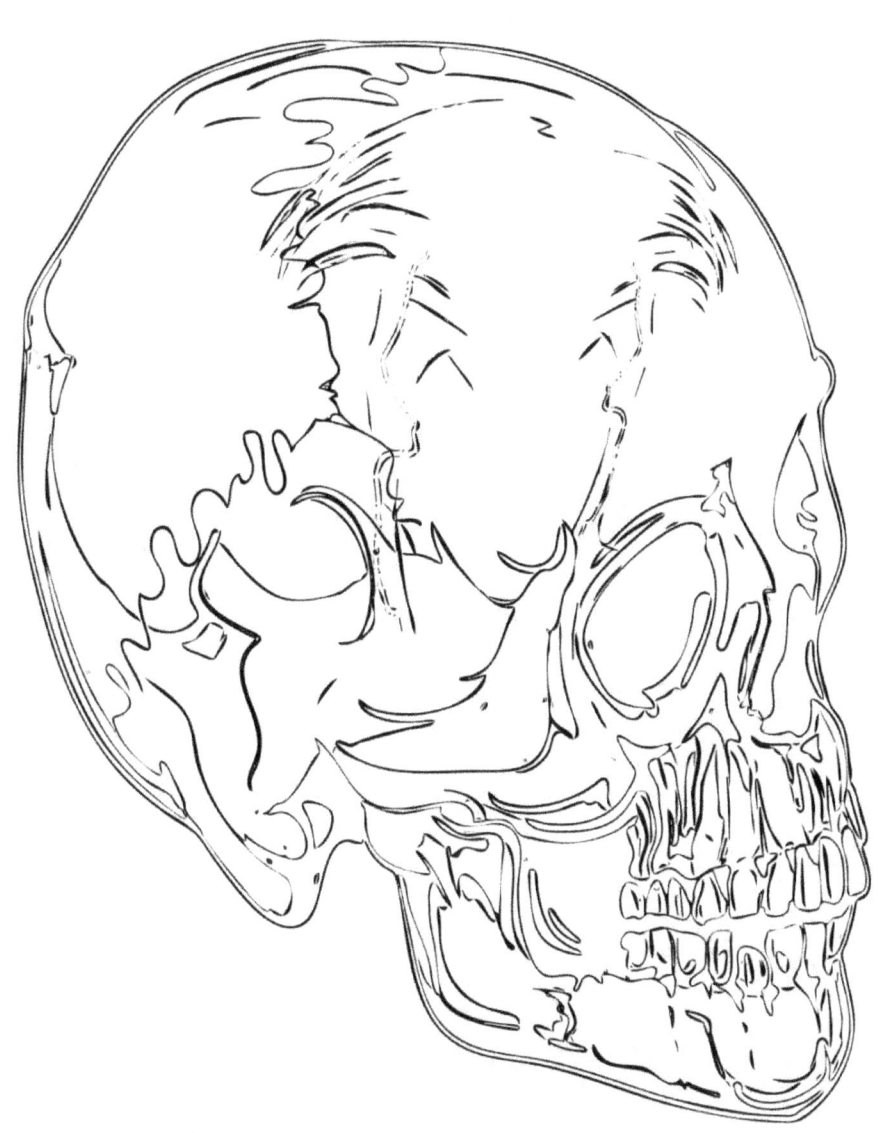

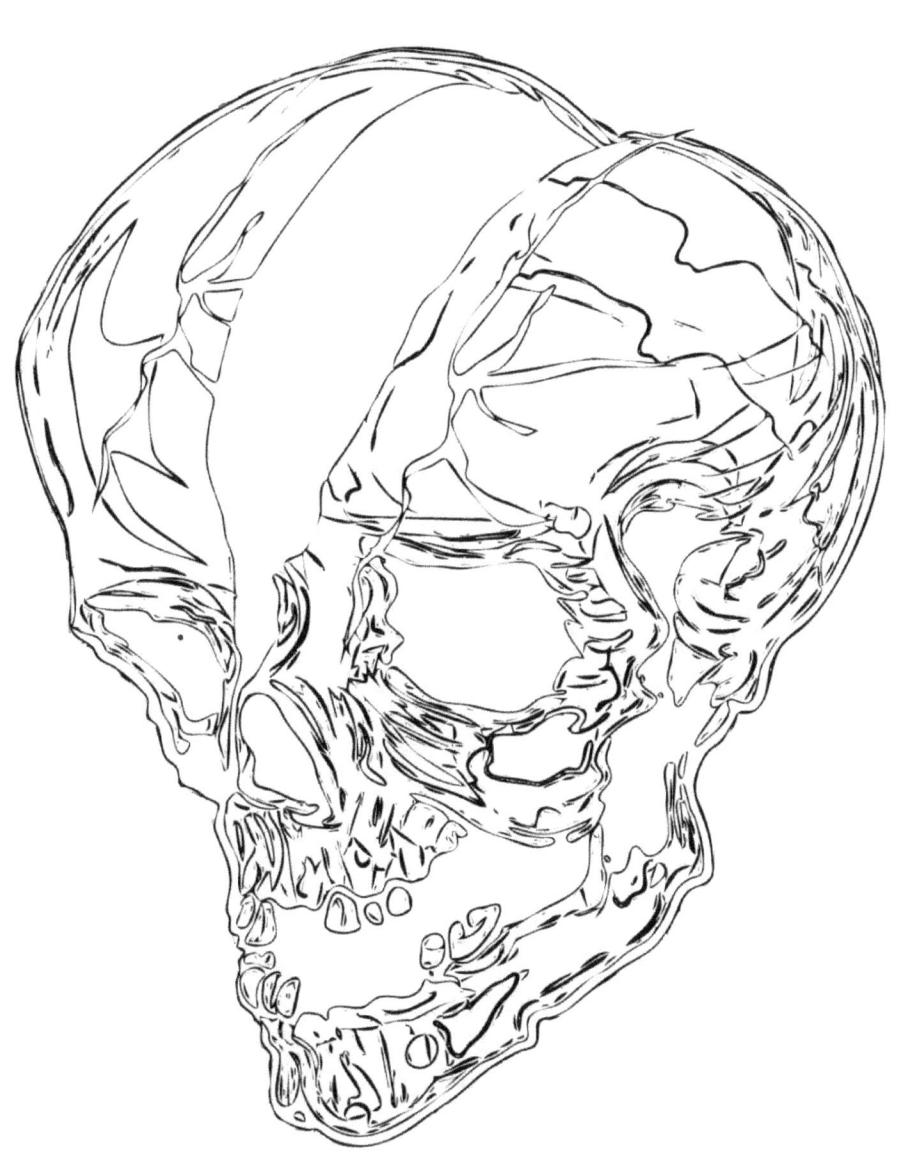

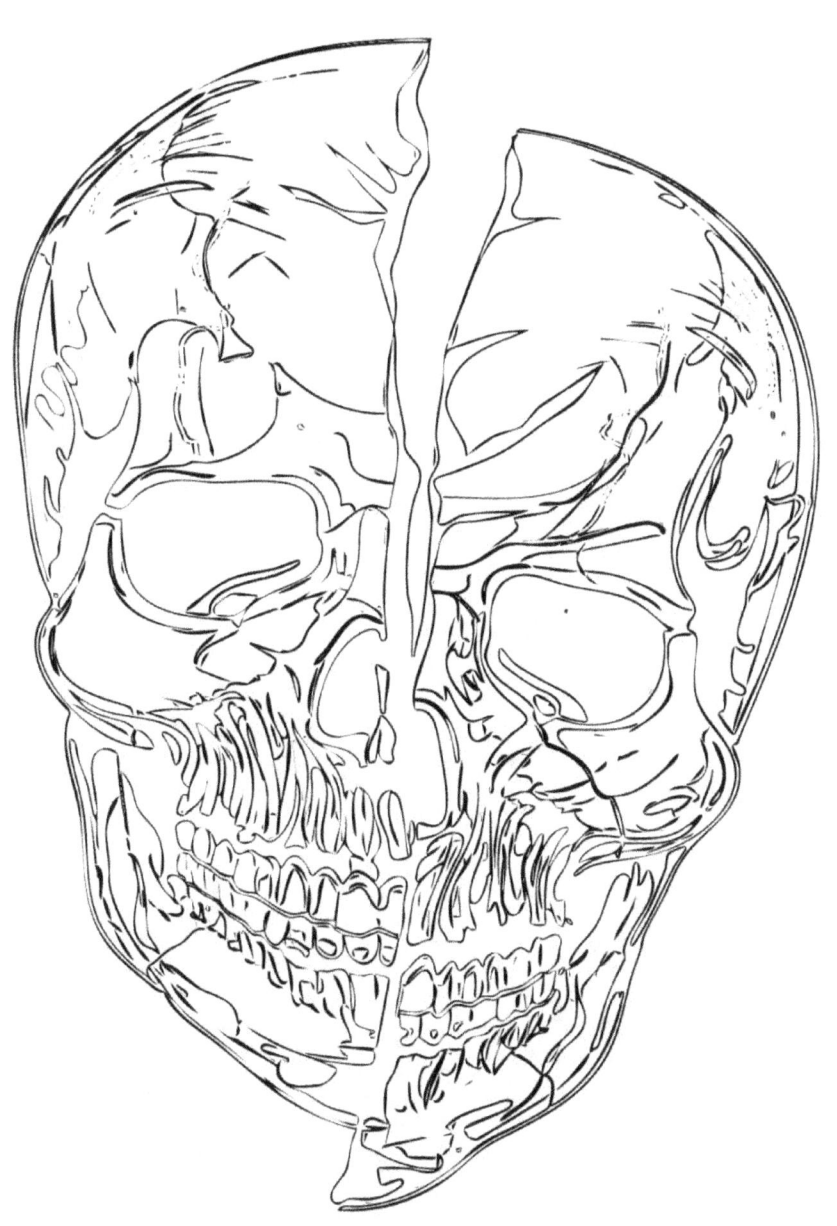

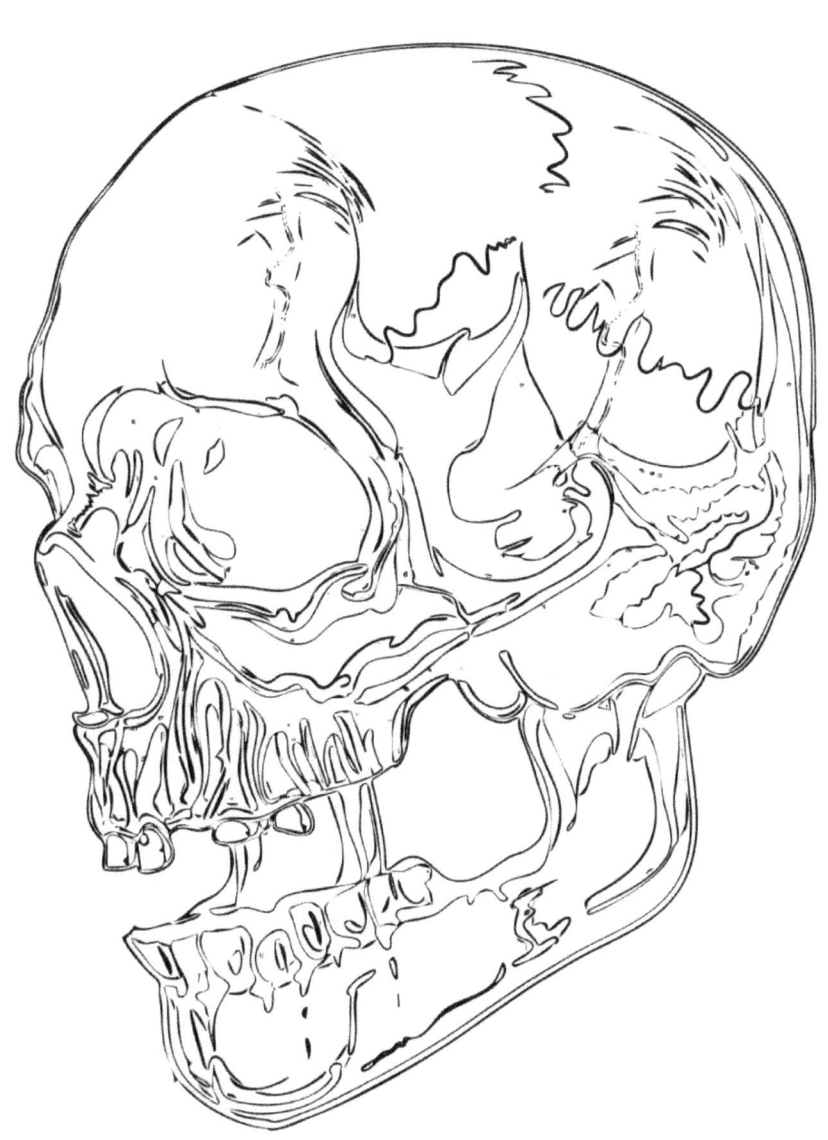

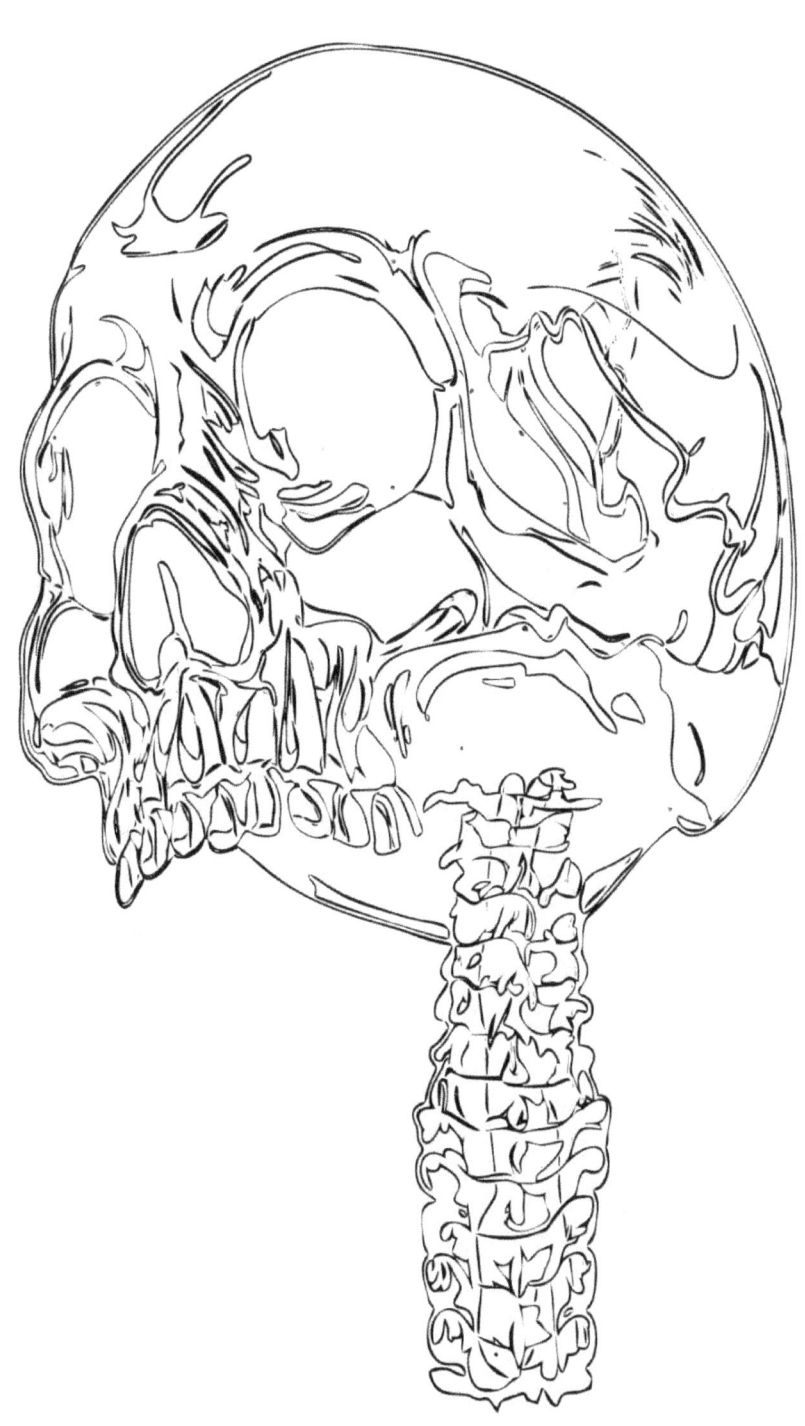

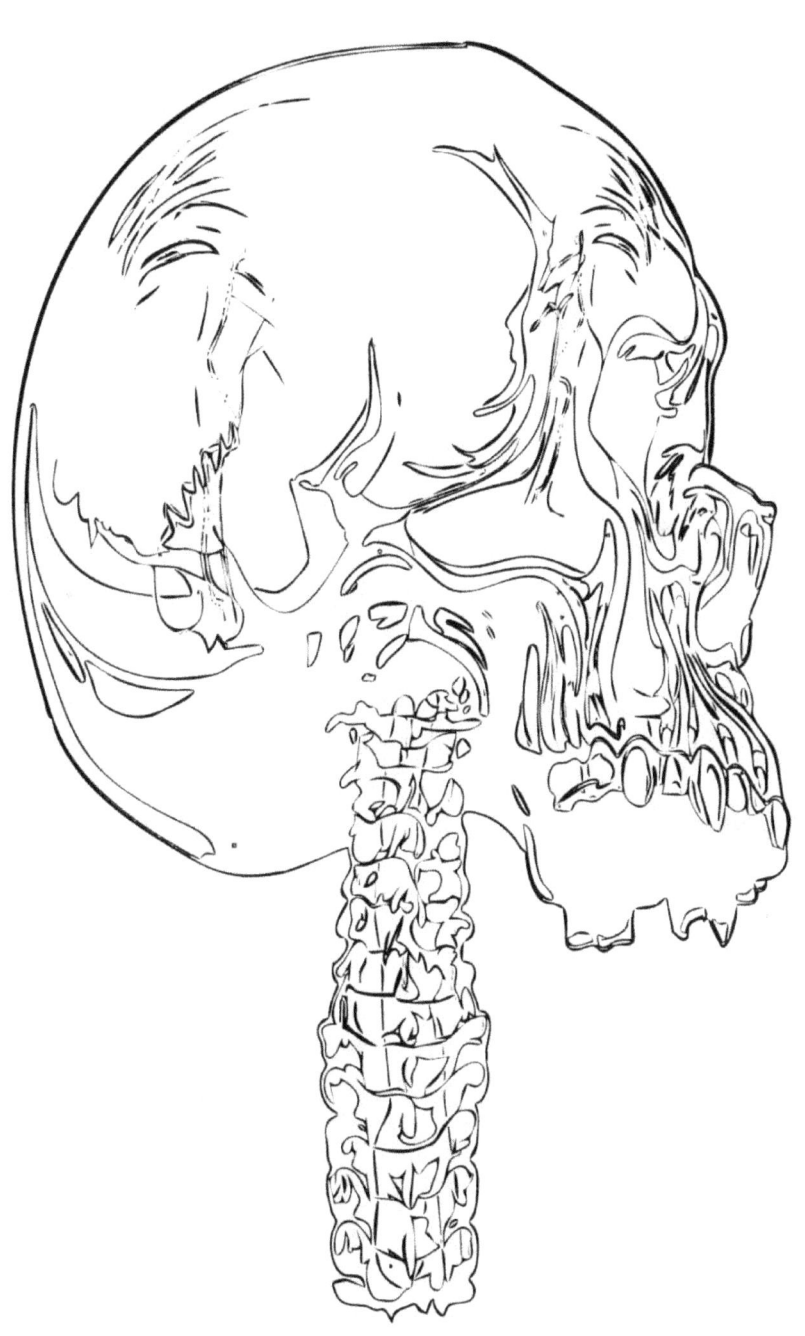

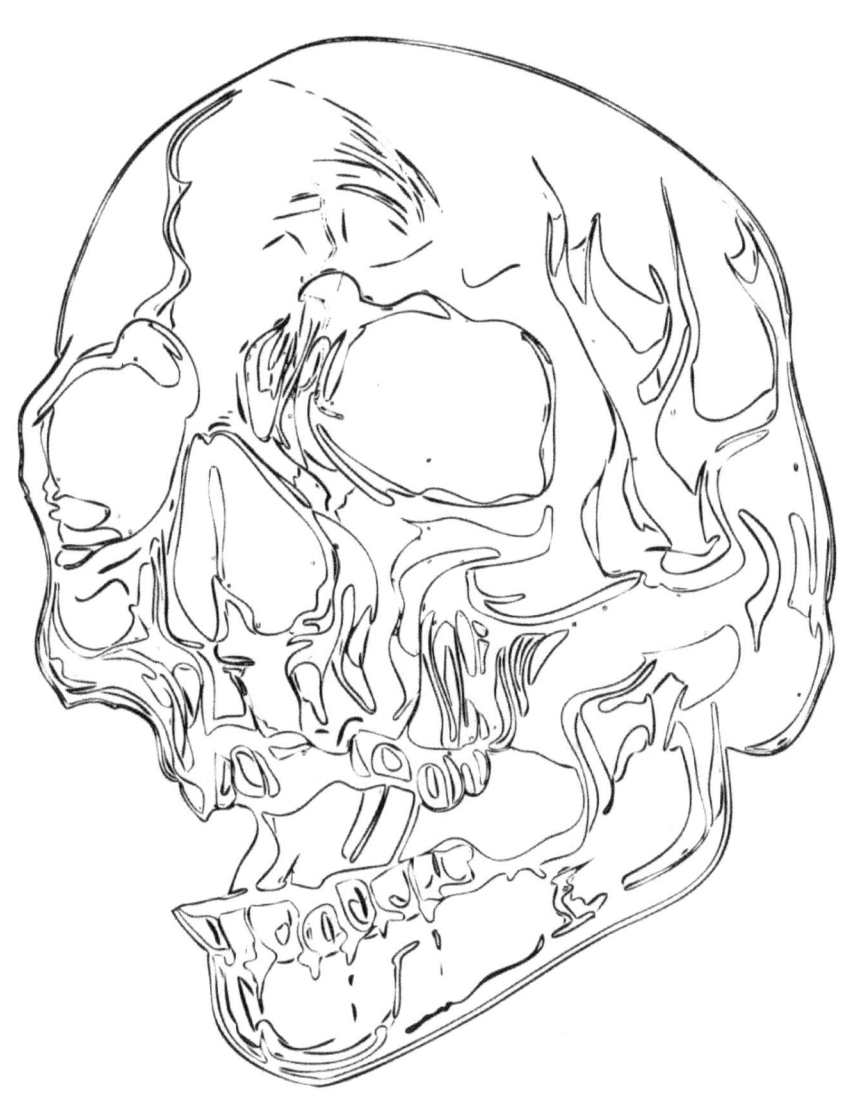

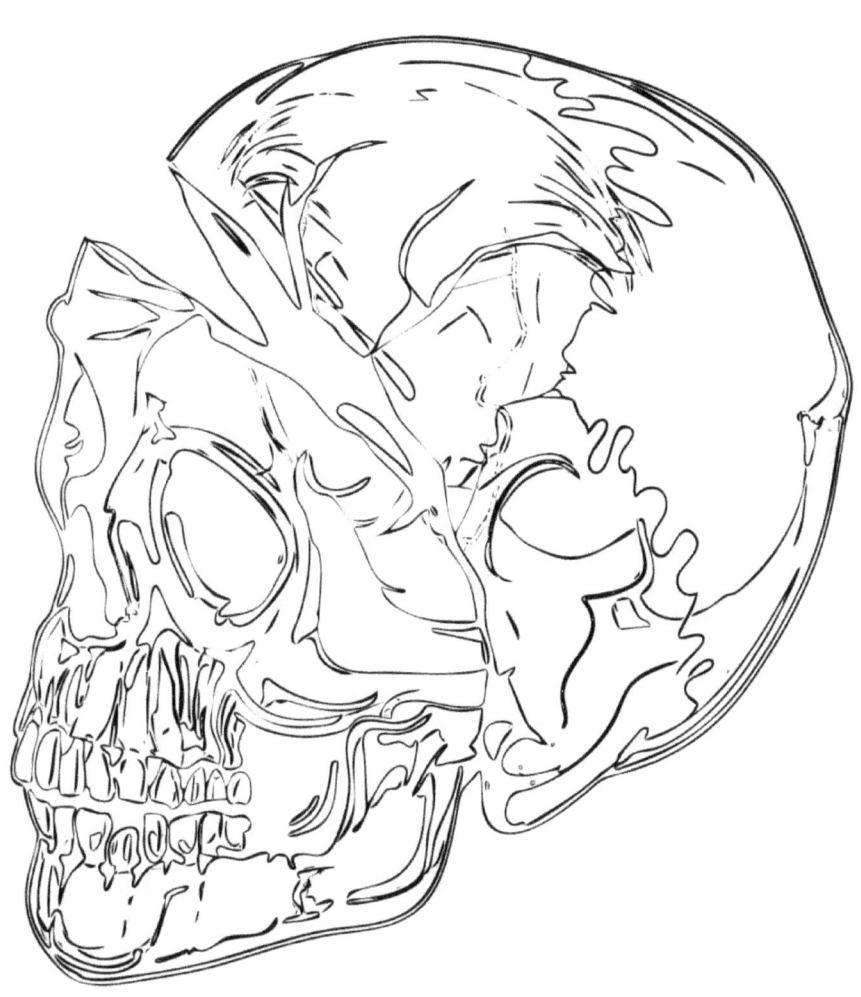

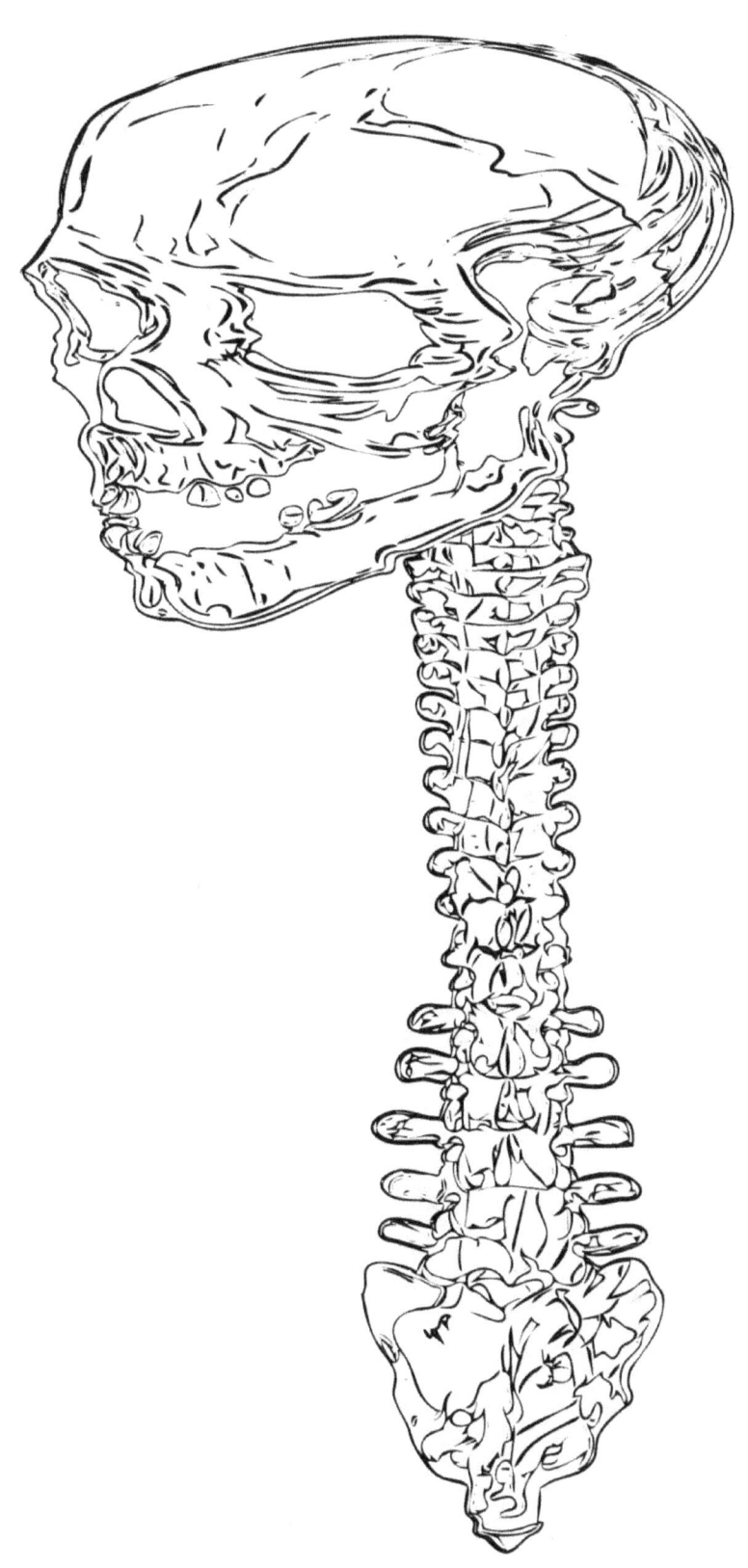

TRIPPIN' SNEAKS
Far Out Sneakers Coloring Book

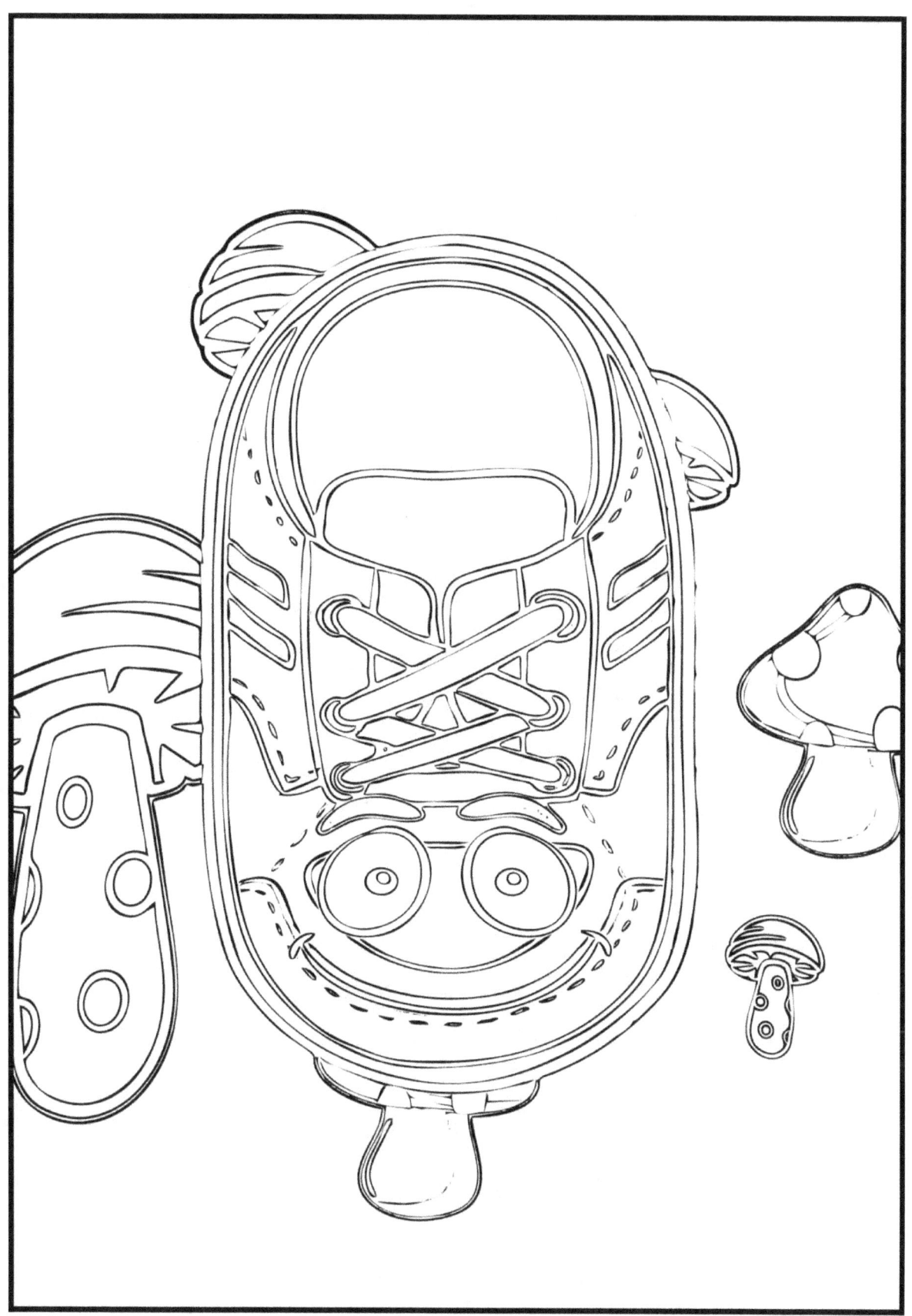

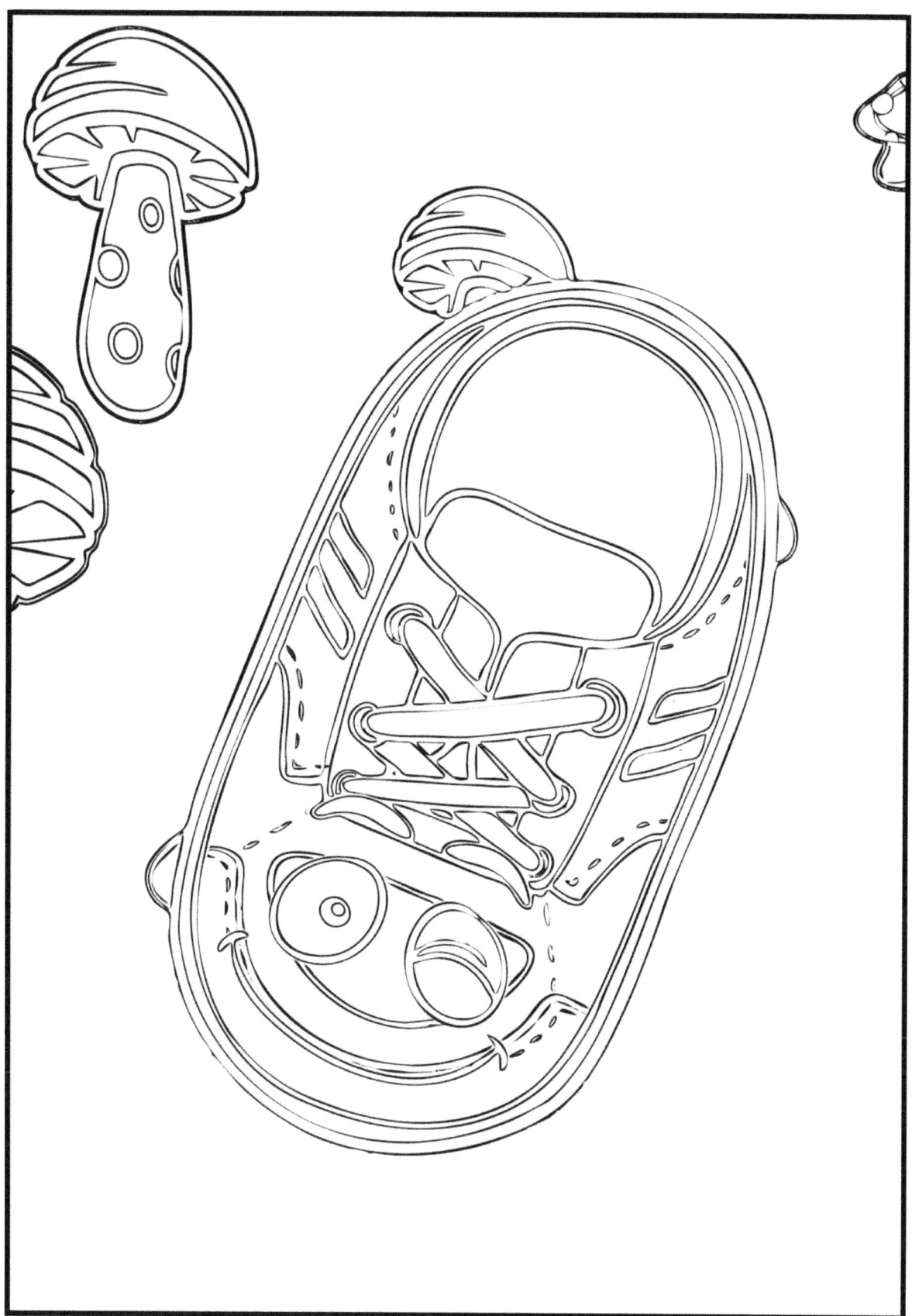

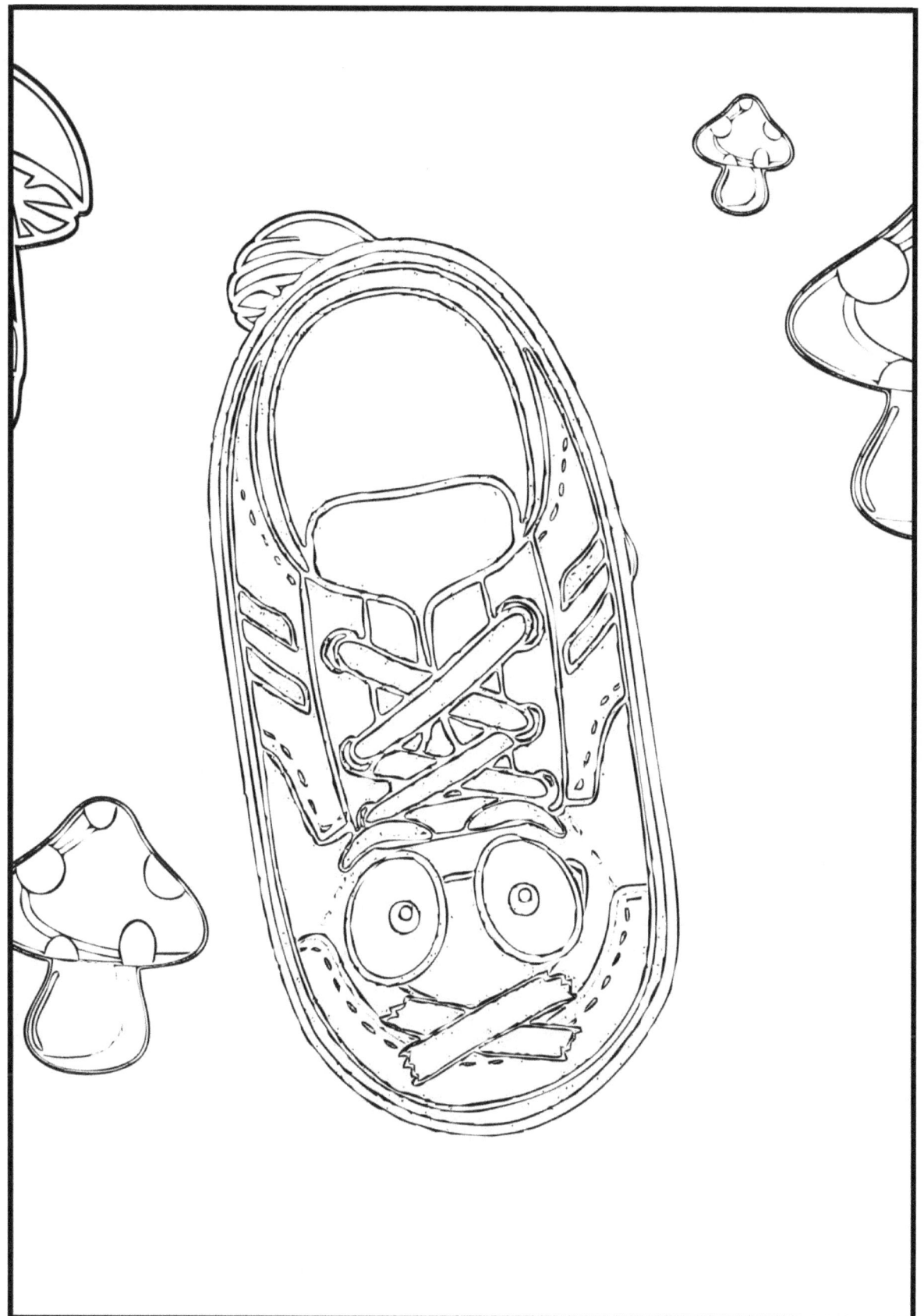

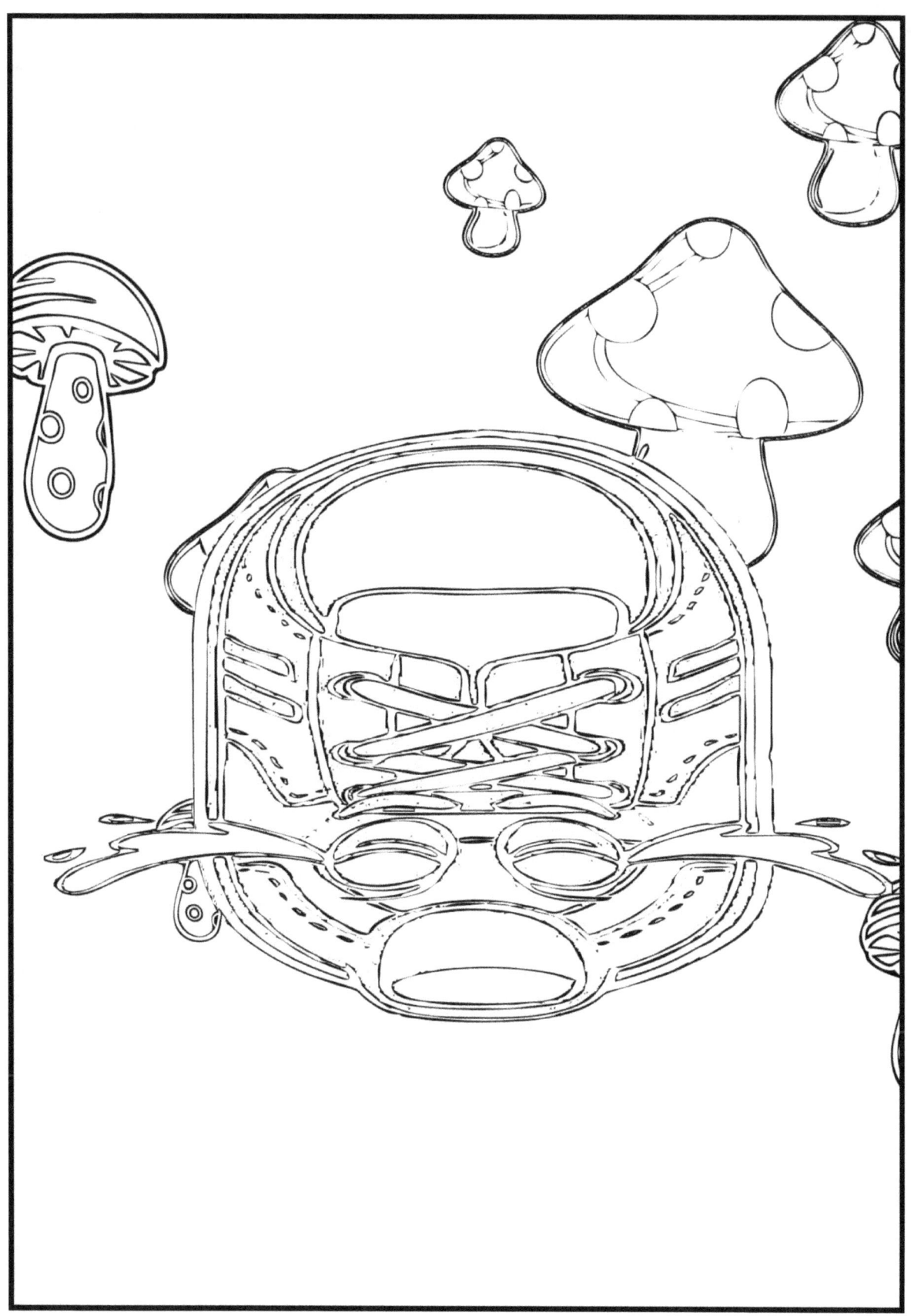

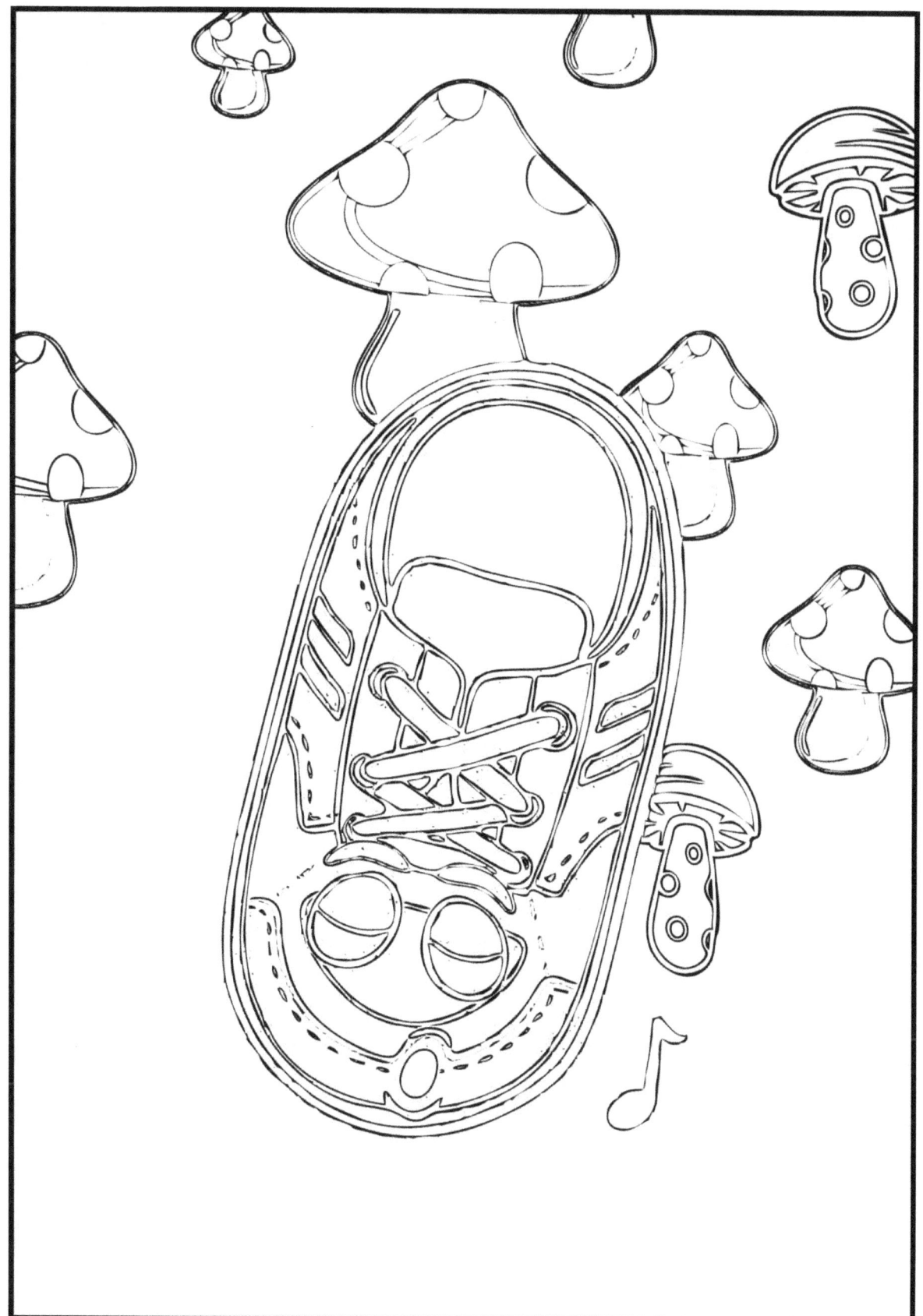

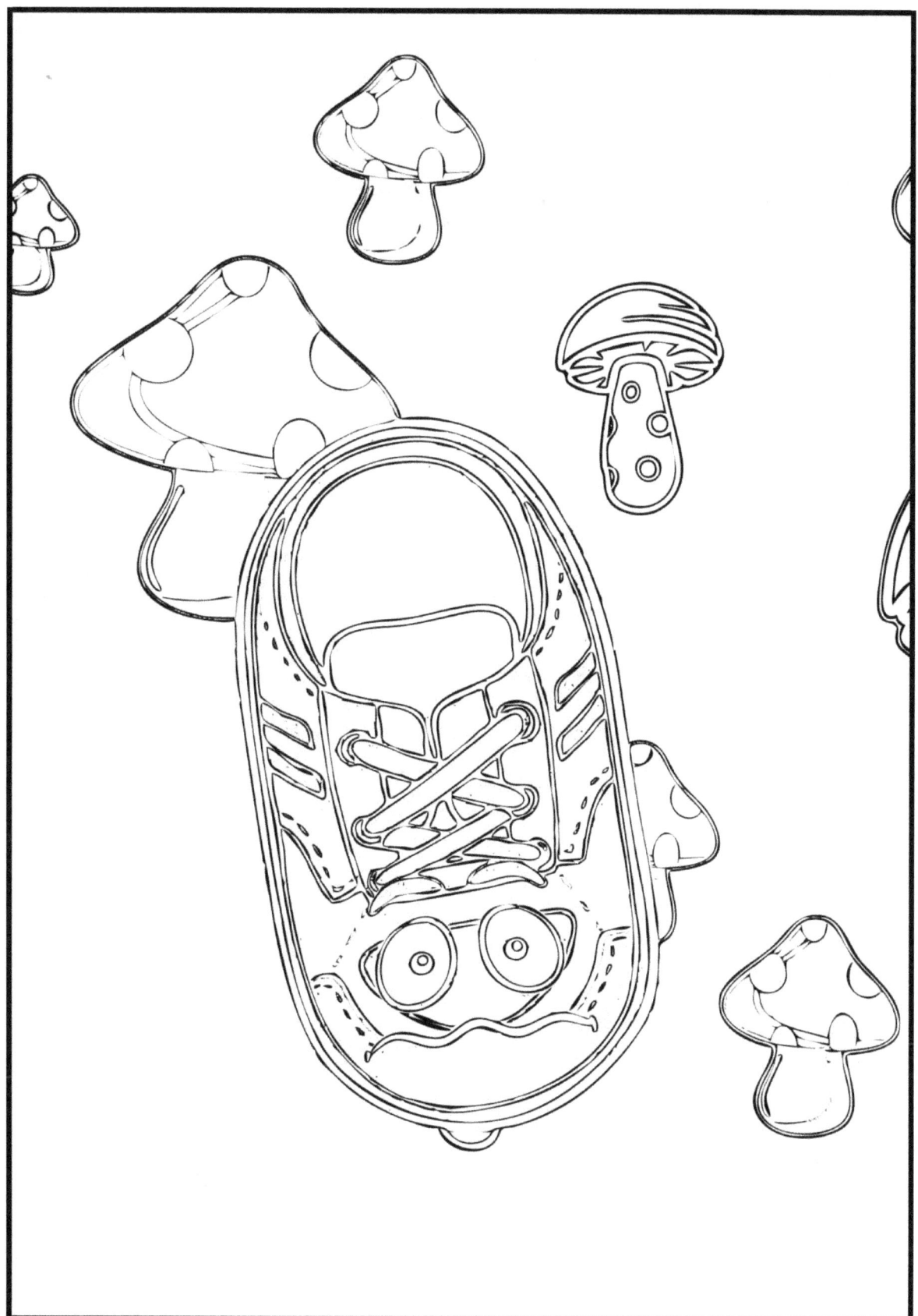

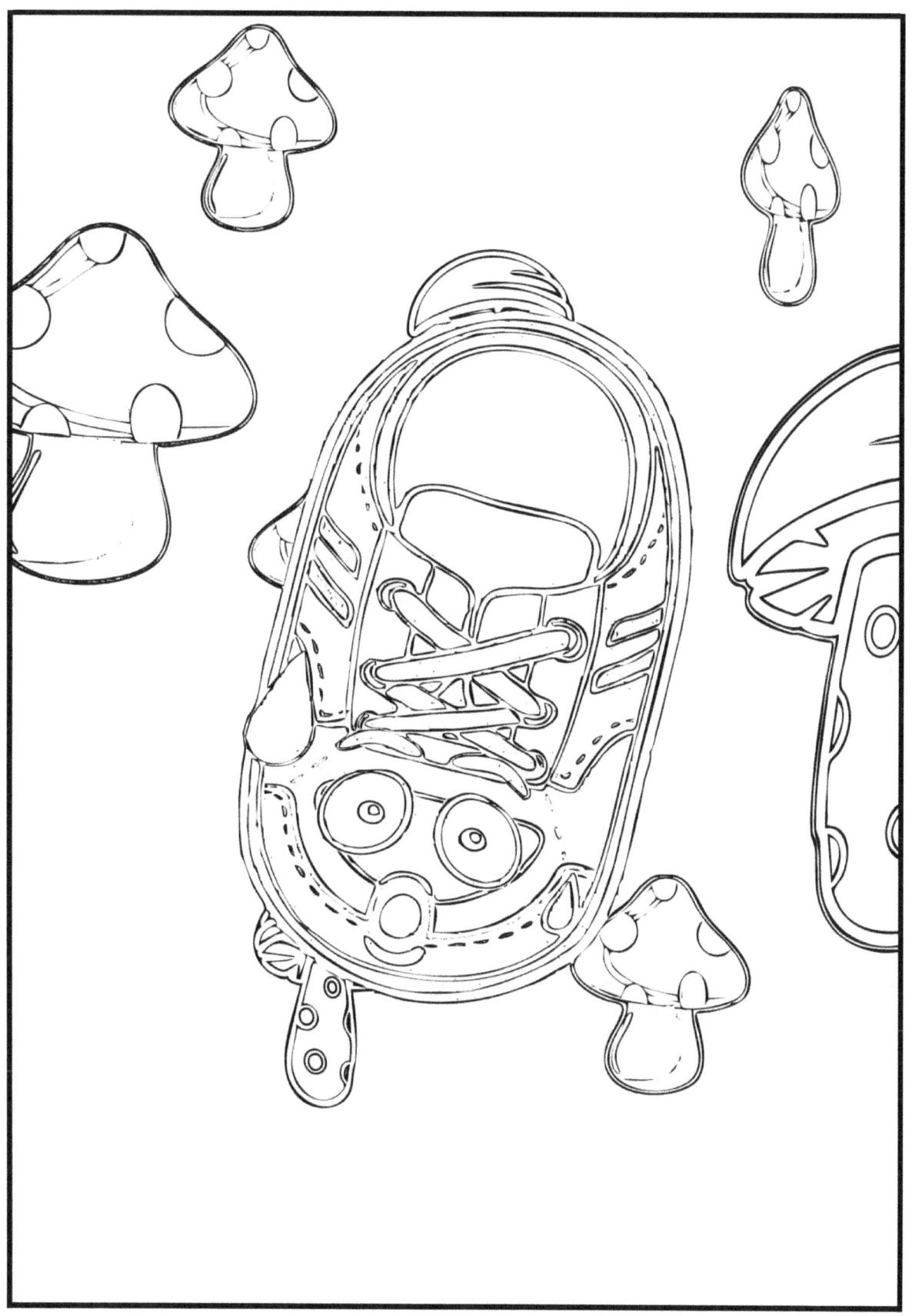

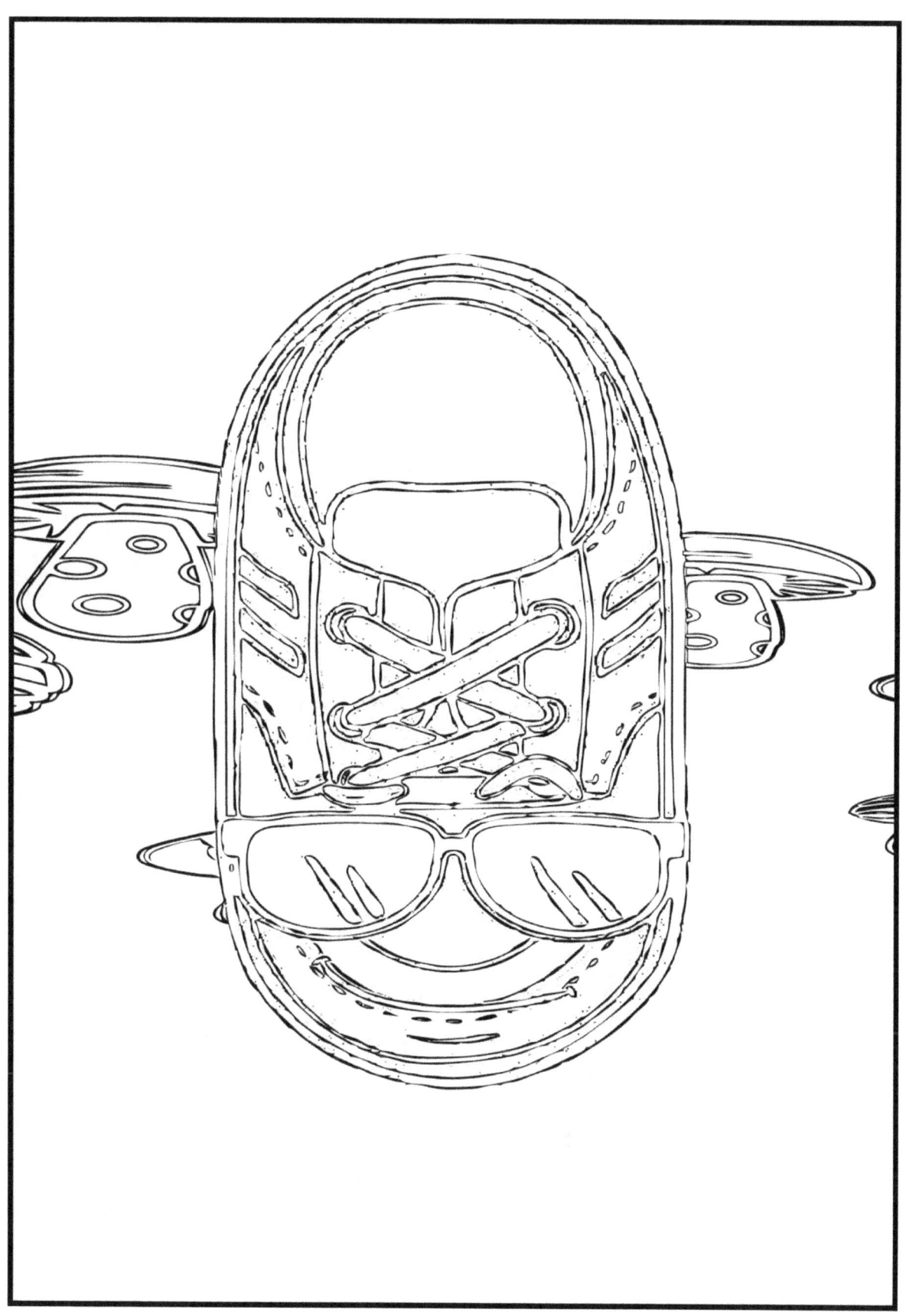

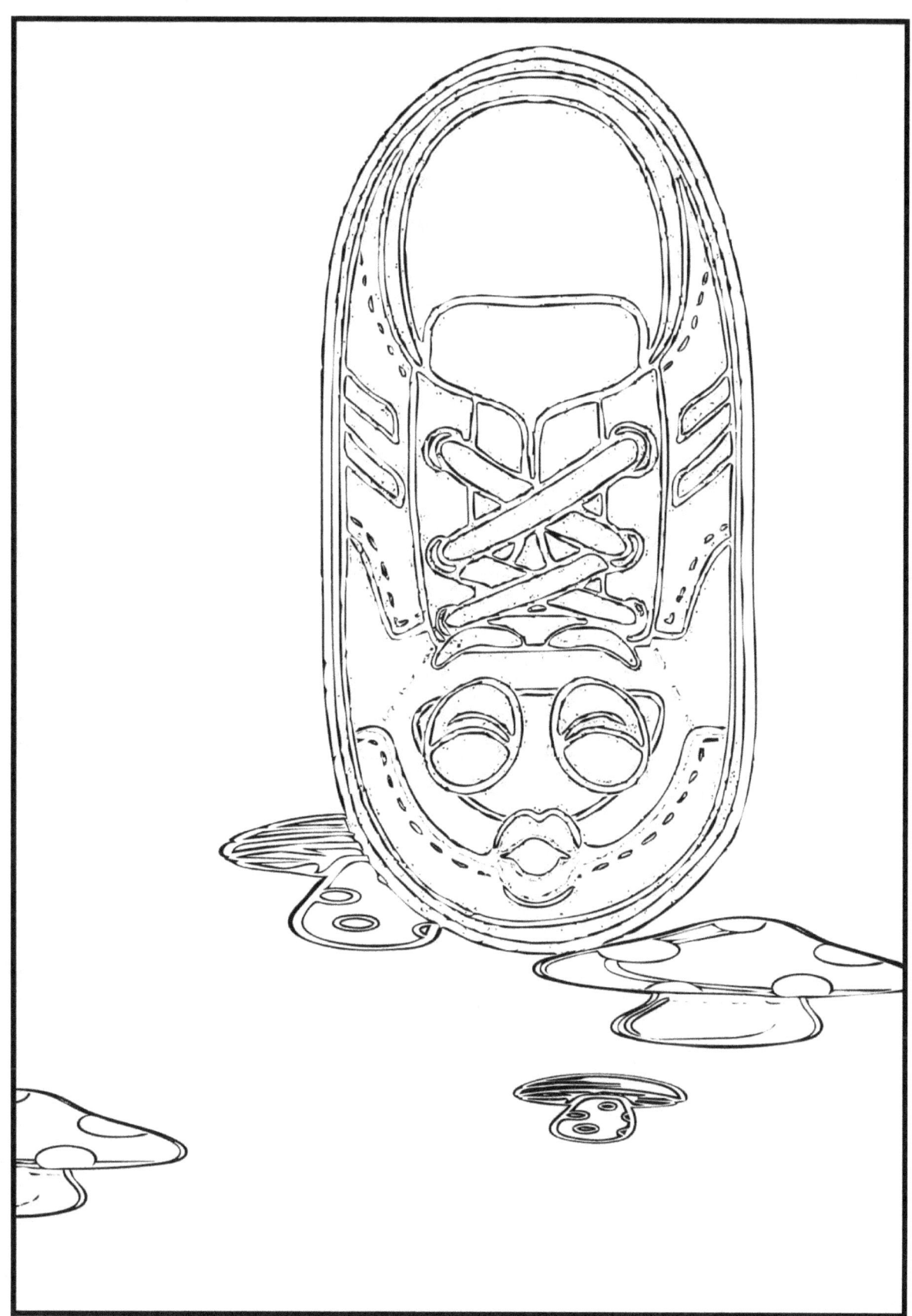

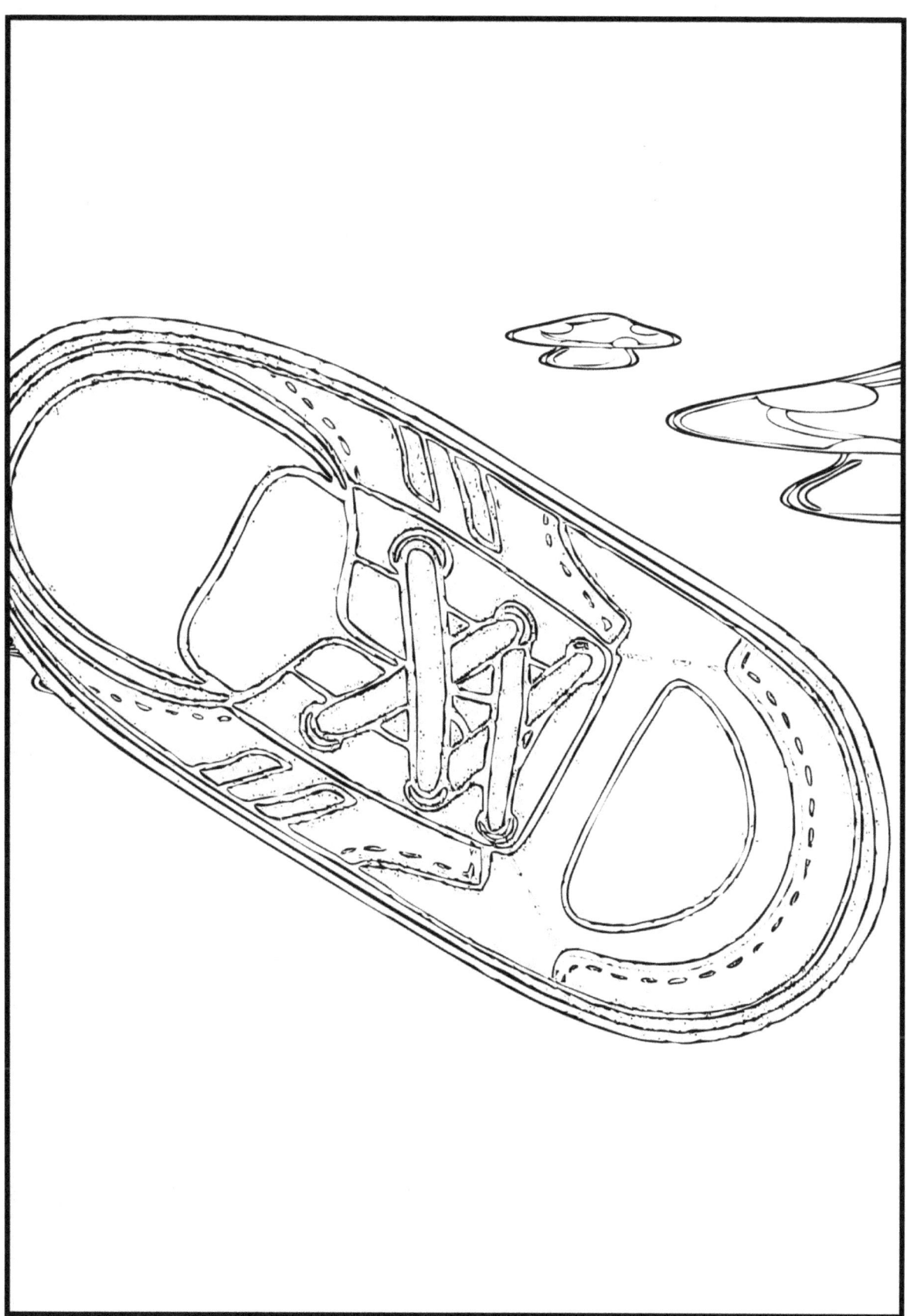

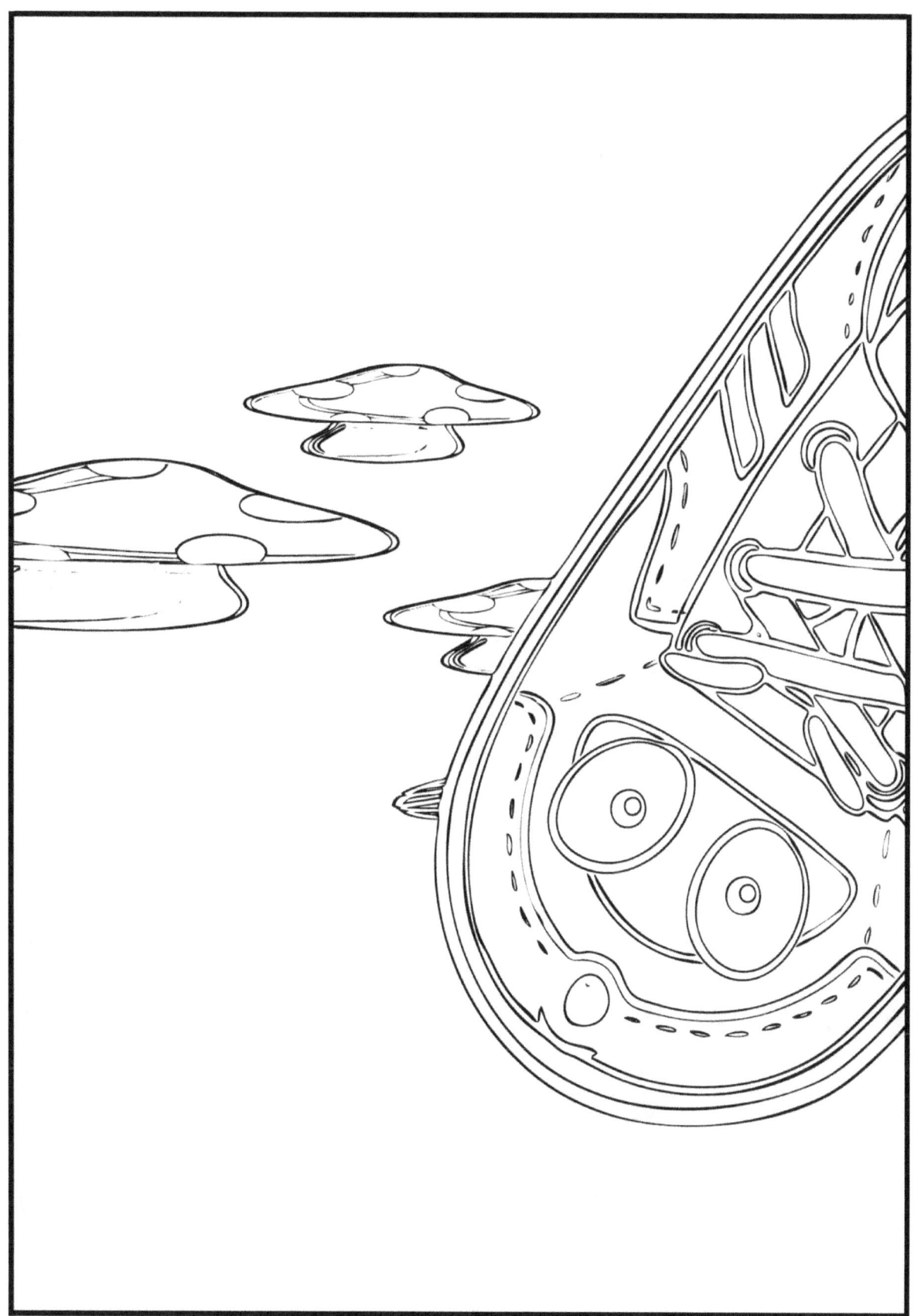

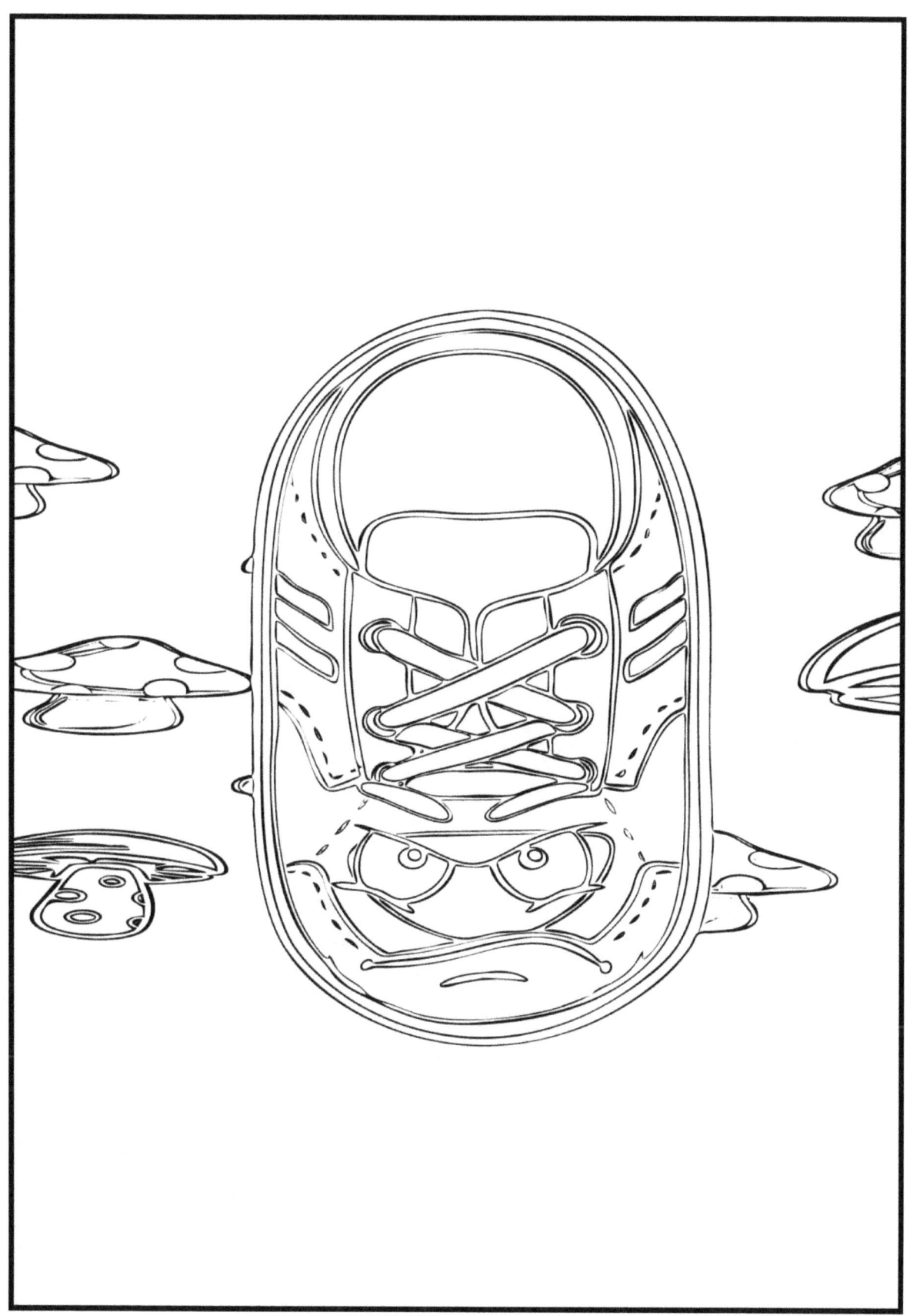

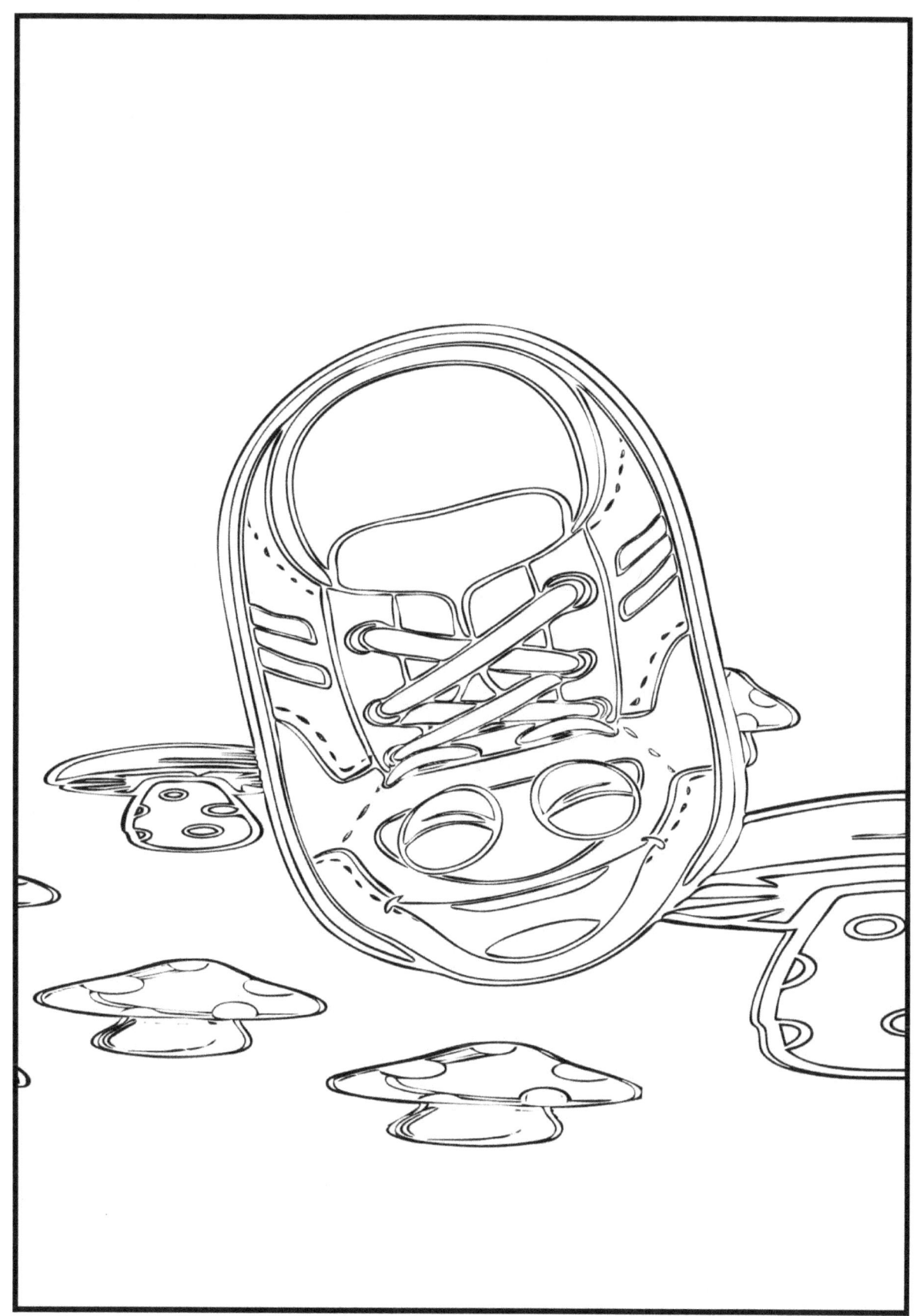

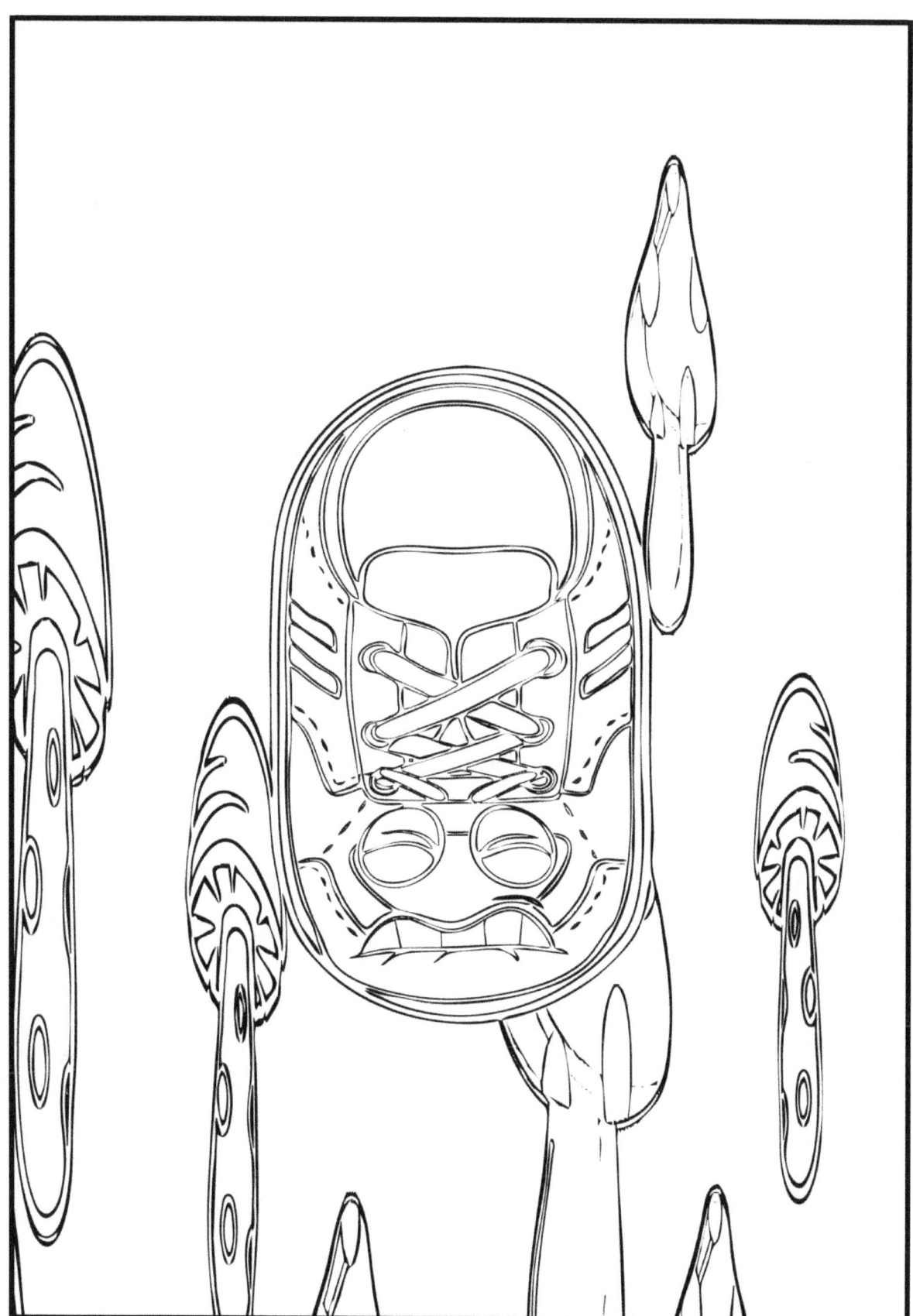

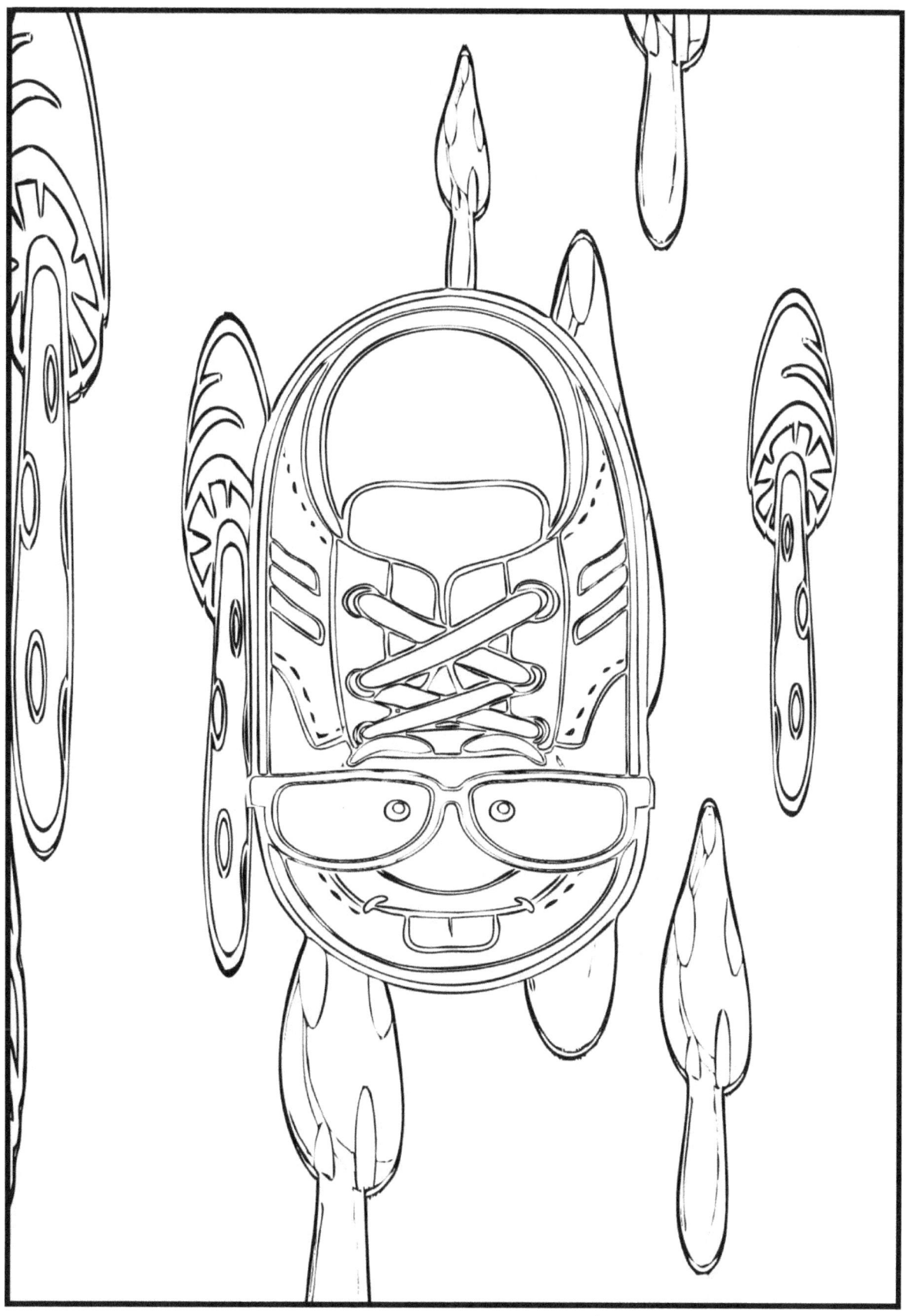

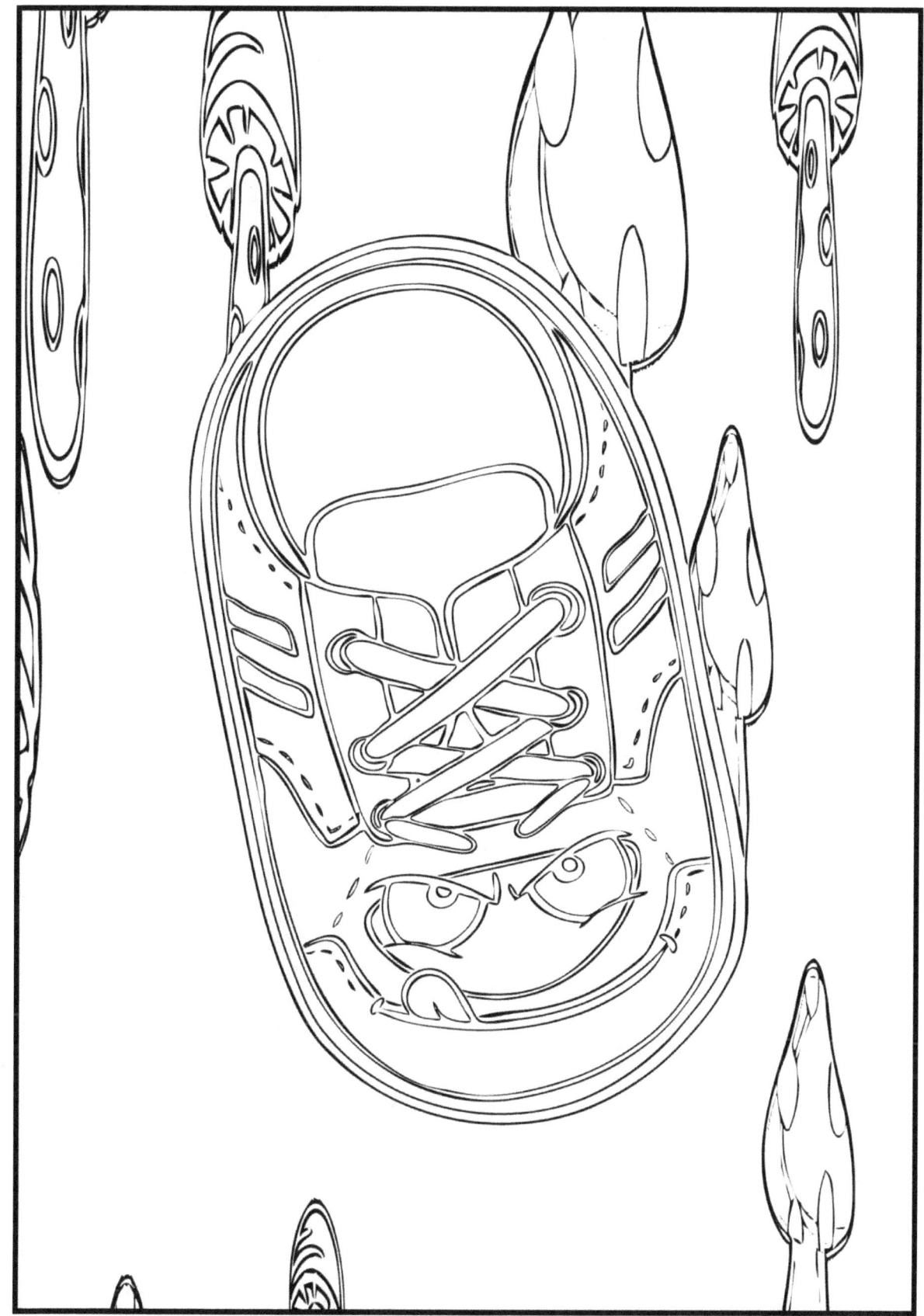

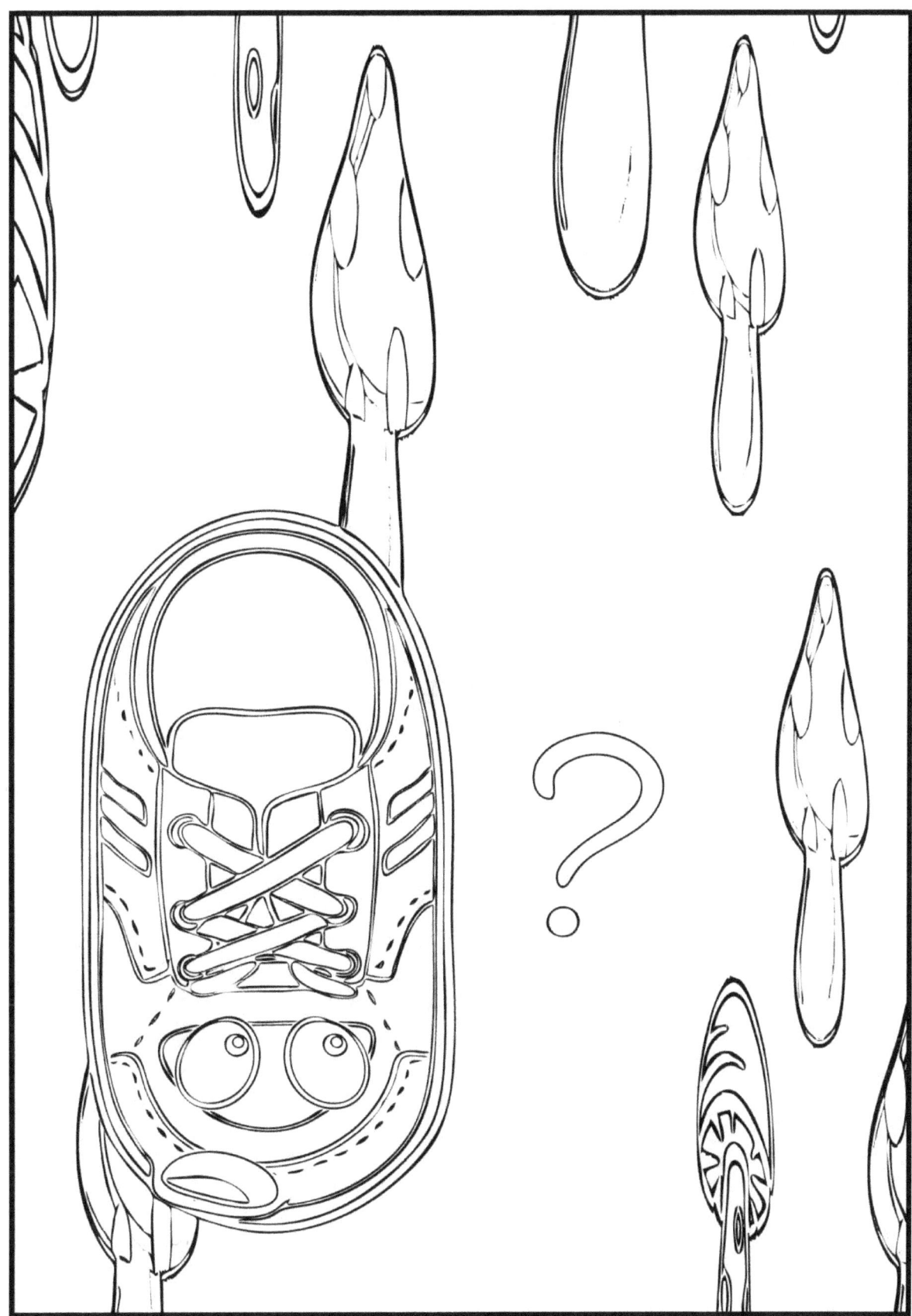

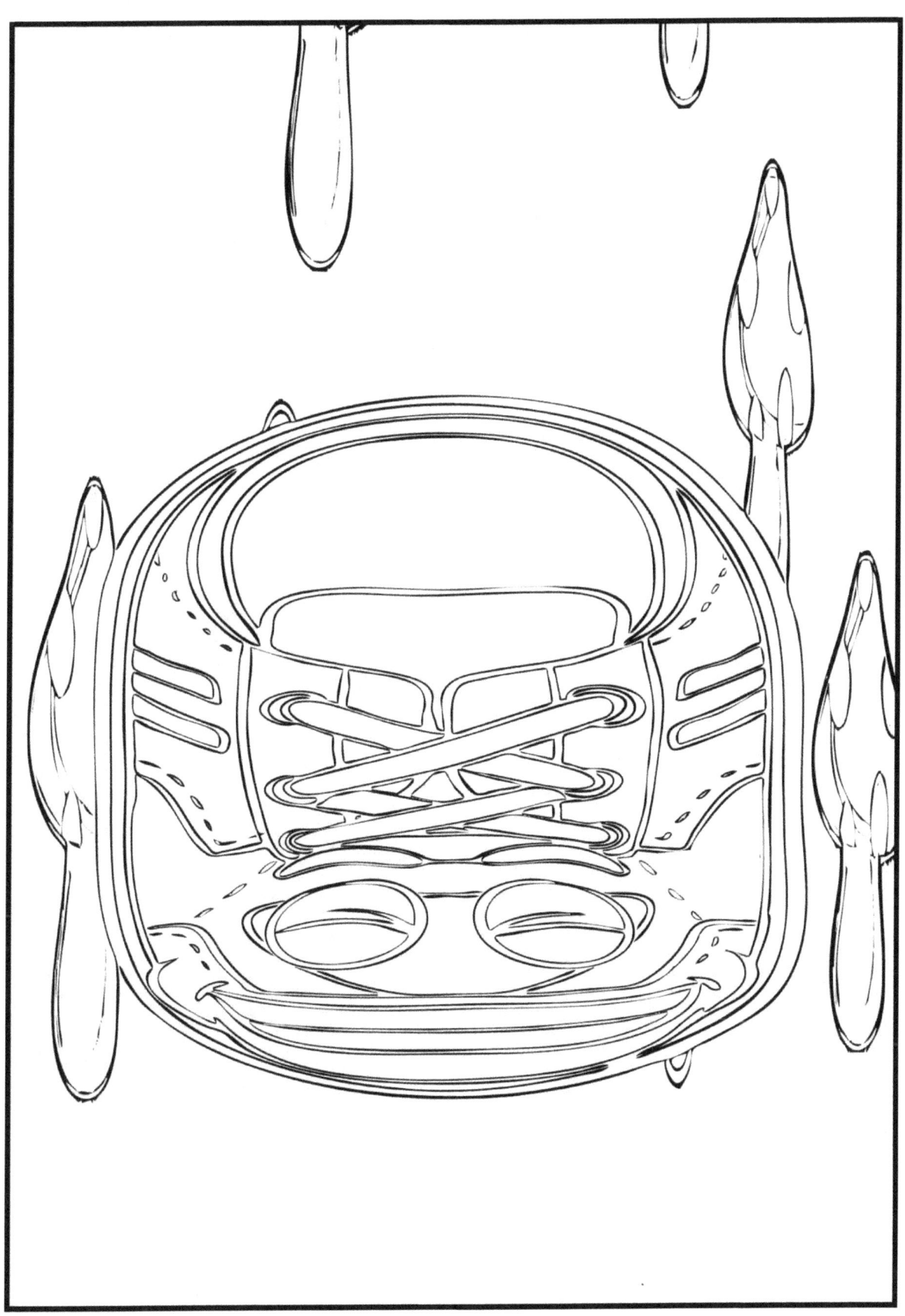

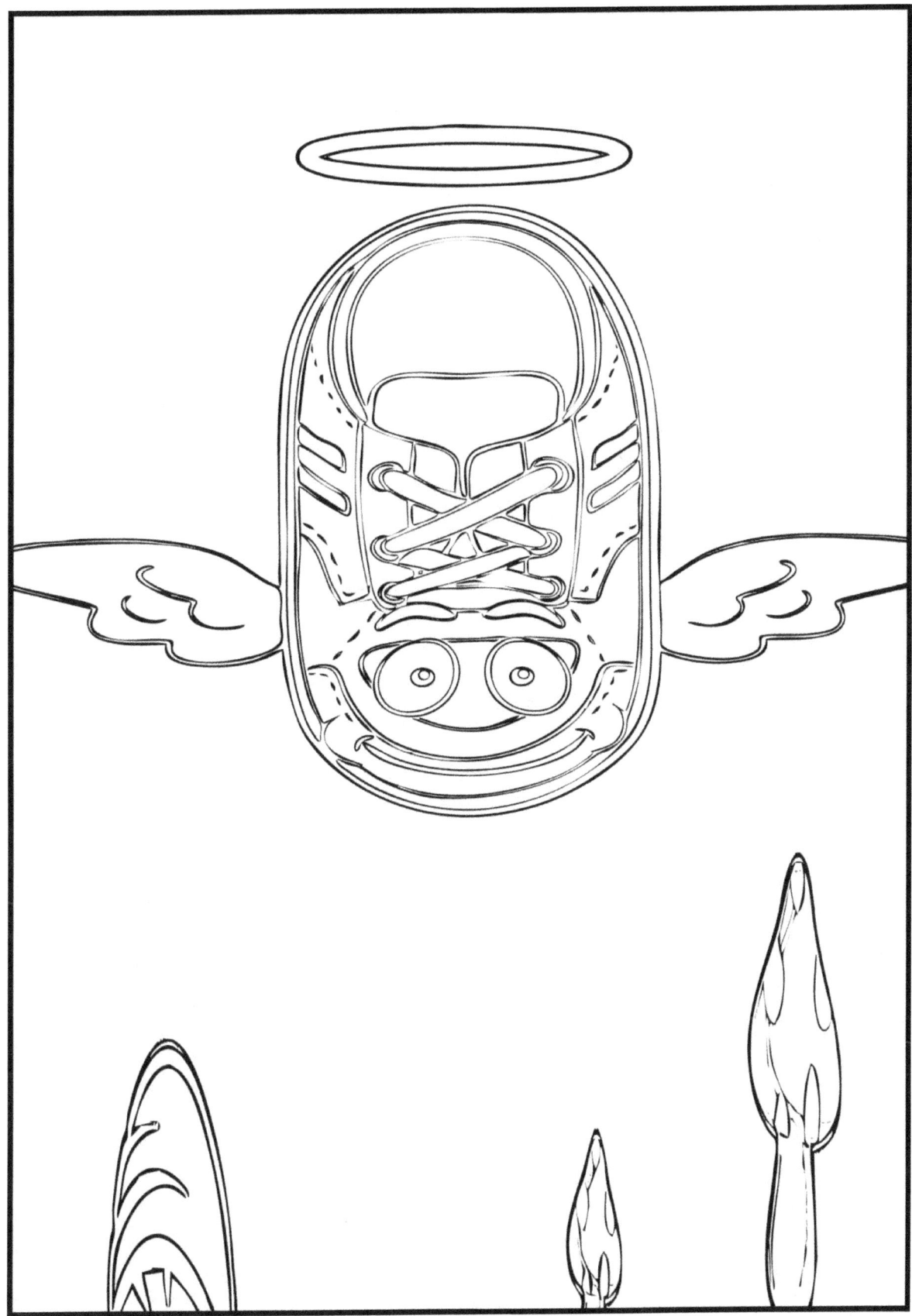

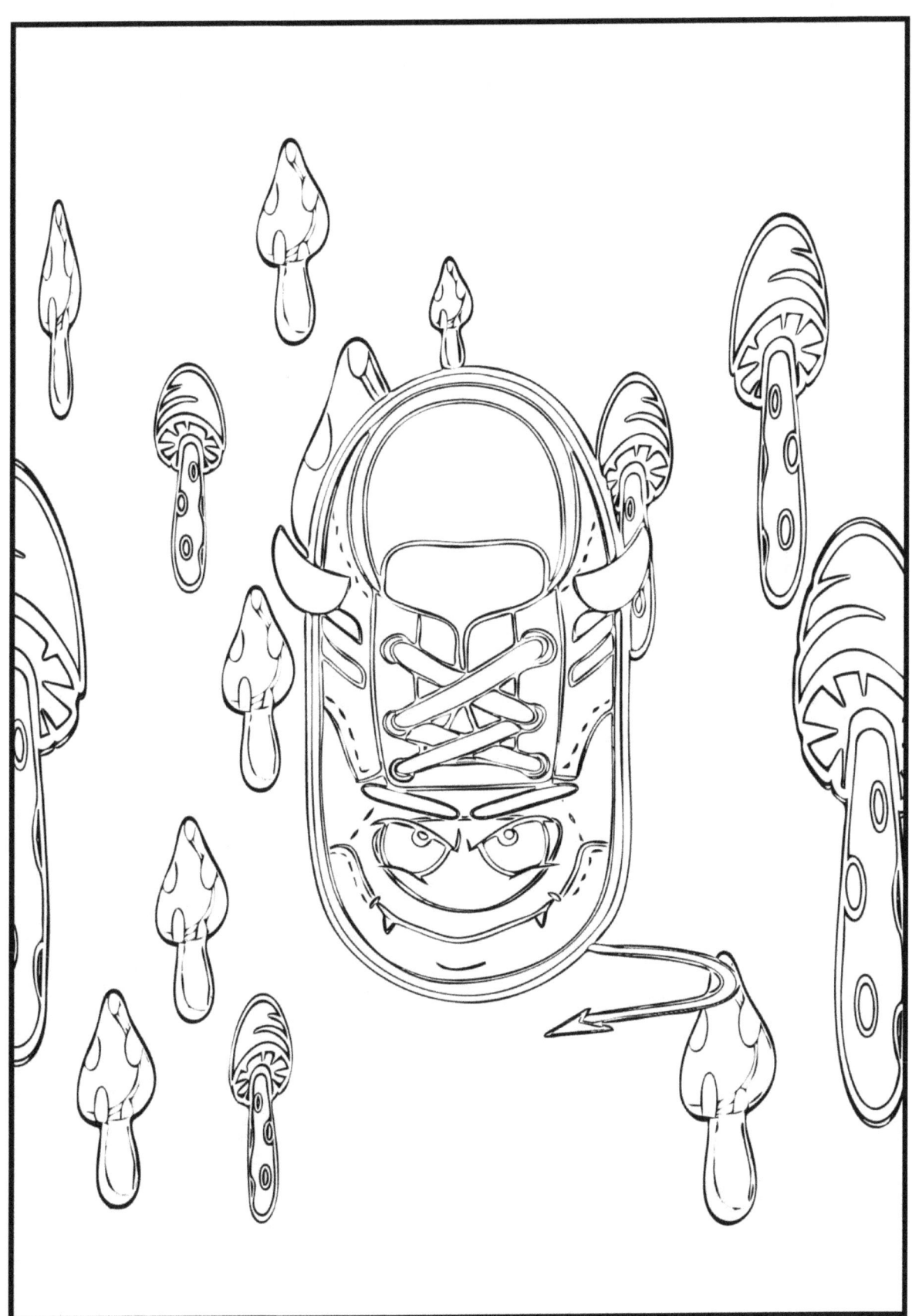

www.ingramcontent.com/pod-product-compliance
Lightning Source LLC
Chambersburg PA
CBHW081600170526
45166CB00009B/2767

* 9 7 8 1 5 1 9 6 6 9 8 6 5 *